TALES OF
A CRUISE SHIP

MARGARET MARSH

Matador
9 Priory Business Park
Kibworth Beauchamp
Leicestershire LE8 0RX, UK
Tel: (+44) 116 279 2299
Fax: (+44) 116 279 2277
Email: books@troubador.co.uk
Web: www.troubador.co.uk/matador

ISBN 978 1783061 426

British Library Cataloguing in Publication Data.
A catalogue record for this book is available from the British Library.

Typeset in StempelGaramond Roman by Troubador Publishing Ltd
Printed and bound in the UK by TJ International, Padstow, Cornwall

Matador is an imprint of Troubador Publishing Ltd

To Selwyn

Contents

Introduction

These stories are the result of diaries I kept from 1998 to 2009 on board ship while my husband was working as Medical Officer with a Norwegian Cruise line. Writing them was a useful way of filling time when he was working and also a method of recording our experiences, especially the places we visited and might want to revisit for a longer stay. They are really a personal cruise log based on actual events, though times and names have been changed to preserve the anonymity of the people concerned. I really enjoyed our cruises to places both far away and closer to home. Arriving in a port by ship is an experience many people never have and for me it presented a taste of adventure in countries I had previously only read about or seen briefly on TV. These 'tales' are brief snapshots of my reactions to some of them and, though too numerous to mention all of the places we visited, I nevertheless hope that they give an insight into a cruising life.

Margaret Marsh

A New Beginning

"Help!"

Black smoke is pouring out of the toaster. The 'pop up' has stopped working, the bread charred and the machine will soon need to be replaced. I had been gazing out of the kitchen window at the birds feeding and had not been concentrating.

Retirement is looming but I'm not sure if I want it. At least, I'm not sure if I want all it implies and I'm not ready for the slippers and armchair scenario quite yet. My husband too, having been part of a rural general practice as a local doctor for over twenty-three years, finds it strange to visualise simply not working any more. So as I pondered on the problems of my ancient toaster and our future, I little knew that a phone call out of the blue that morning was about to change our lives for the next ten years.

I watched my husband becoming more and more animated as he answered the call. The proposition comes from a cruise company that employs family doctors as medical officers on short-term contracts. He's invited to join the team because there is a gap in the list and someone is needed at short notice for a cruise to Norway. To my great delight I'm invited to go along as well.

Later that day, I looked at my wardrobe and rapidly discarded almost everything in it. Having always associated cruising with glamour and sunny blue skies, my holiday clothes all looked too shabby, too warm or too small and there was no time to lose weight. A visit to the hairdresser was the most pressing need, and was quickly achieved. Afterwards, feeling more confident, I took a realistic look at the contents of my wardrobe. Spread out everywhere they gave a jumble sale air to the spare bedroom but, with the help of a fashion-conscious friend and a bit of mix and match, we decided I only needed to buy two new posh frocks for formal evenings, a sun hat and some deck shoes. After all, this might only be a 'once in a lifetime' experience. With a gleam in my eye, I planned a shopping spree.

The doctor's wardrobe is easy. His uniform is provided for him, so he only needs a few casual clothes for going ashore. The one ominous item on his list was a warm woolly hat for the lifeboat. Why would he need to go in a lifeboat?

Having sorted out the clothes we then had to find something to put them in. A hunt in the loft produced a battered selection of dusty old cases already full of long forgotten items that might come in handy some day. These will certainly not do. Another visit to town and we bought a very large, green case on wheels that later turned out to be a big mistake. I had enthusiastically thought we could get everything in one large case but, of course, I'd forgotten all the little things we surely couldn't do without. These included the small electric kettle for making tea in our cabin when we don't want to be sociable. Later I learnt that the crew call it 'having a night in'. Then there was a hairdryer, shaver, laptop (to be carried separately), sandals to wear by day and by night, and both black and white shoes and black and white belts to be worn with uniform. The small spaces in the case were filled with cameras, mobile phone, makeup, suntan cream, wash bags, bow ties, seasickness pills and all the jewellery I could find, beg or borrow. Inevitably another small case was needed and a rucksack for shore days. Travelling light was not for us, I'm afraid.

Arriving at the port on the day of departure was exciting because it was completely different from anything we had ever done before. First of all we had to fill in forms and complete formalities in the cruise terminal. Large identity badges were pinned to our jackets and we set off towards the quay pushing our luggage down a long path crisscrossed with metal tracks. The wheels on the case kept getting stuck in the tracks and we had to stop several times to lift it out. The ship towered above us and looked enormous from the quay. The crew gangway was a long metal staircase, not at all like the glamorous entrance used by passengers, and by the time we had pulled and pushed the suitcase all the way up, we arrived at the entrance looking slightly dishevelled and breathing heavily. We were ushered through the X-ray doorway and signed in once again by a burly Philippino officer. "Welcome aboard, Doc," he said with a smile. From then on, to my amusement, my husband is known as Doc and I'm often Mrs Doc or Ma'am, like the Queen!

While the Doc went to meet the rest of the medical team, I decided to use the lift to go down to deck three and find our cabin. It wasn't easy because the sides were swathed in protective material in readiness for the piles of suitcases arriving later. I had to feel around behind the stuff to reach the lift buttons and, at first, found myself going up instead of down. Crew stewards and stewardesses were rushing around preparing the cabins for the afternoon's new intake of passengers. Pulling my wheelie suitcase behind me, I apologised as I got tangled in the cleaner cables and tried not to knock over the piles of clean sheets and towels in the narrow corridors. The doctor's cabin was at the end of another passage behind the medical centre and the hospital. This area is not carpeted and leads to the crew restroom and the mess where they eat all their meals. I found this out because I opened all the wrong doors until I eventually reached our room.

The cabin was a pleasant surprise. Although not as smart as the passenger cabins I had glimpsed on my way, it was large, carpeted, and had a double bed. There was a leather settee and an armchair, a TV and a fridge. The furniture was old but looked comfortable and curtains screened off a section of cupboards to make a hanging space for clothes. The adjoining bathroom had seen better days and some of the floor tiles were cracked but I thought as long as the water was hot and everything worked we should be all right in the ablutions department. Through the two portholes I could glimpse the feet of passing dockworkers. We were right in the bows of the ship a few feet above the waterline.

After some lunch together, the Doc went on some other medical mission and I set off to try and find my way around the ship. The long corridors on each deck all looked the same so I kept getting lost. I found the library and then the pool deck. One attractive lounge/bar called the Observatory has wide picture windows all around, but when I tried to show the Doc later on we got lost again in the maze of corridors. It was going to take some time to learn 'fore and aft, port side and starboard'. I was curious about doors labelled 'Crew Only' and we slipped inside one to explore these areas forbidden to all but the ship's workers. It was like another world behind the glamorous parts of the cruise ship. Metal staircases spiralled upwards to the officers' mess or led down to lower decks where the crew lived and all the stores were kept. Later, when I got to know some of the crew, I would be invited to use their ironing-room or shown where to find milk in one of the small pantries behind the scenes but, I quickly learned to use these privileges with discretion and usually only with the Doc nearby.

We went on deck to watch the passengers coming aboard. The disabled or those with children came first and then a small army of wheelchairs arrived. I tried to gauge which passengers looked fit and healthy and who might be the Doc's first patients in evening clinic. Regular cruisers were easy to spot because they looked relaxed and chatted happily to each other and the crew. Others looked harassed and tired, perhaps because they were apprehensive or had travelled a long way to get to the port. Later on in our new career we realised that these few hours incognito are the best part of each cruise. We could just be passengers like everyone else, having afternoon tea and cakes while eyeing up possible friendships.

At 5pm the engines rumbled into life, the deck vibrated gently below our feet, ropes were cast off and we slowly pulled away from the quay. The white cliffs of Dover glowed in the evening light and a little pilot boat bobbed gently alongside us on a calm sea. It seemed a perfect way to begin a new way of life.

Learning the Ropes

Before every cruise begins, there is a lifeboat drill and everyone has to take part. I wait for the signal to find the way to our muster stations; seven short blasts on the ship's siren and one long one.

At the bottom of the narrow wardrobe in the cabin I found a red lifejacket and struggled into it. It was rather like wearing a red plastic box with a stiff collar that keeps your head upright but obstructs the view of your feet, and had a light which didn't seem to work and a whistle on the end of a piece of string. As advised by the instructions on the back of the cabin door, I dressed warmly, struggling into thick trousers and a woolly hat, then set off down the corridor and up three flights of stairs, huffing and puffing. I felt as though I was losing weight at every step. In the Neptune lounge, an officer trying not to smile told me that it was unnecessary to dress in warm clothing for a practice drill.

Gradually the room filled up and everyone was bumping into one another and apologising. Urged on by the baritone beat of the siren, an old lady zimmered a pathway through the red sea of lifejackets. Soon, we were all given a lifeboat number and were directed to a designated area of the lounge. I greeted my fellow survivors, who found my woolly hat irresistibly funny. I don't tell them I'm the doctor's wife and we all stopped smiling as we listened to instructions on what to do if the need to abandon ship should arise. "If it becomes necessary to jump," the burly Norwegian officer said in a loud sombre voice, "pinch your nose with one hand and hold down the lifejacket with the other so that it doesn't flip up and choke you when you hit the water." He illustrated this manoeuvre with gusto and I wondered if I would remember to do it all while taking the fateful leap? Afterwards, I wasn't the only one who needed rescuing from the lifejacket. Unfortunately I had tied the cords so tightly that I couldn't escape. There is an amazing number of ways knots can be tied and untied and when we finally untangled the strings and checked our lights and whistles it was time for a well-earned cup of tea. Drill turned into quite a friendly social occasion as we all asked each other, "Where are you from?" and " Is this your first cruise?" Regular cruisers eagerly provided information on everything from the best restaurant for fresh breakfast croissants to interesting shore tours not to be missed.

Back in our cabin the Doc asked how I got on. I gave him an edited account leaving out the woolly hat and the knots and directed his attention to the next new experience: the uniforms hanging in the wardrobe. As temporary valet, I did the first wardrobe inspection to see what was hanging there. When I become more experienced I will know that the jacket with old egg or wine stains down the front probably belonged to the doctor who was there on the last cruise. If it's almost new and looking most attractive, then sure as fate it's not going to fit. One jacket's buttons will not reach the buttonholes; another has sleeves long enough for a chimpanzee, while none of the trousers are ever designed to accommodate middle-aged paunches. There is another danger point concerning the uniform of the day, a one in four chance of getting it wrong because of the variations of black, or black and white, with a selection of long or short or no jacket and long ties and bow ties. On cruises to warmer climes, tropical white becomes the order of the day with white canvas shoes which, though cool, are difficult to keep clean. A printed timetable (always getting lost!) dictates when each uniform is to be worn. Sometimes panic strikes as, just before the Captain's cocktail party, the bow tie won't be tied or the spot shifter won't work. Once, sometime after our first cruise, I was forced to sprint down the corridor in pursuit of the Doc, who could be seen in the distance wearing black socks with white shoes, and another time, shame and horror, the epaulets on upside down!

Soon after we arrive on each cruise, the Doc takes the uniforms down to the tailor on the deck below to be altered in time for evening surgery or collects a new selection to try on. There isn't a great deal of time because he must be dressed and ready for evening clinic. On this, our first cruise, we didn't know the routine of course and needed some gentle guidance from the nurses, waiting to show him around the medical centre.

I unpacked and went to find the ironing room for my crumpled frocks. Ironing itself is no easy task because for some strange reason the irons in the passengers' laundry were chained to the ceiling. Perhaps it's to prevent the passengers secretly walking off with them or to stop them falling on your toes when the ship gives a sudden lurch. Complications arise when you're halfway along the ironing board and come to an abrupt halt at the end of the chain. Should you iron all the bottoms or all the tops of the trouser? In rough weather, while fighting to stay upright and turn the garment round at the same time, you may lose control of the iron and it's highly likely to swing back and brand you with its hot, shiny bottom. Perhaps it would be a better idea to use the passenger laundry service. There, somewhere below decks, clothes are immaculately washed and pressed and returned to the cabin on hangers, by a pink-faced steward with damp and frizzy curls, who looks as if he has come straight out of a steamy Jacuzzi himself.

There was a small notice in our bathroom that asked passengers to help save the environment by reusing towels if possible. "Please place towels you would like replaced on the floor." The trouble is our stewardess was determined we should be thoroughly clean and dry at all times. However many times I hung up our towels they were all replaced twice a day used or not. After a few days I decided to hide them in a drawer but forgot to tell the Doc who then demanded fresh towels from the mystified girl. I also resorted to hiding the kettle because rumour had it that crew were not allowed to have them in the cabin. Cups and teaspoons also got whisked away to a galley somewhere so behind the hanging garments in the wardrobe sat a box for hoarding them along with all my secret comforts.

One of the Doc's comforts has been smuggled on board secretly too. I felt that first impressions are important and that maybe we should leave the bottle at home but the Doc was adamant that a wee dram now and again might come in useful.

Consequently, a bottle of Highland Grouse, for medicinal use only, had found its way into our small fridge via a large carton of liquorice allsorts. The sweets had been donated to a worthier cause: the nurses' sweeties jar in the medical centre. All this subterfuge was later found to be unnecessary. We would find that most of the things we craved were easily available on board.

One morning, a day at sea, my curiosity about the mysterious area below deck was rewarded. We went below to the bottom of the ship, the bit the passengers and most of the crew never see. Going through yet another 'crew only' door I had not noticed before, we descended in a battered, rattling lift that groaned and shuddered as it slowly creaked into the depths. When we got out, Alberto the First Engineer was waiting for us and signalled us to follow him. It was too noisy to talk and he handed us small plastic bags containing little yellow earplugs. I dropped one of mine while fumbling to push it in my ear, hoping he hadn't noticed. I would never find it on the floor in the dim light down there. He opened a heavy, sliding door and a blast of hot air hit my face as we entered a throbbing metal maze of pipes, tubes and machines.

Trying to adjust to the cacophony of sound, I found myself moving like a robot along the narrow passage. Peering down, I deliberated about where to put my feet and clung to the safety handrails with both hands. The soft lights cast shadows and it was difficult to see obstacles underfoot. I felt the raised edge of a metal plate beneath the soles of my trainers and trod warily. Climbing up a narrow iron ladder, our guide pointed a warning finger so that we didn't bang our heads on the unseen hazards above. Coils of pipes ran along the low ceiling, disappearing into boxes and then appearing again, to wind their way into yet another humming piece of machinery. Wherever the passage got wide enough, the engineer stopped and we all collided gently. Because I couldn't hear a word he was saying, I watched his lips intently as he described the water distillery tanks, the engine that runs the stabilisers, the engines that make electricity, and the engines that make every other engine work. Most awe-inspiring were the glistening pistons in the centre, relentlessly thrusting forwards and backwards. Beside them, men in blue overalls, their faces shiny with sweat, wiped their hands on oily rags and smiled proudly, as we passed. I wondered what it must be like to spend whole days working down here, especially when the sea was rough.

As the last sliding door slammed behind us, I shuddered at the thought of being left behind it and heaved a sigh of relief. These doors can be automatically locked to seal off parts of the ship, should water get in or fire break out, thus limiting the damage to one area. I thought of the young seamen who waved and smiled at us as we passed them and hoped they would never get trapped inside.

Facing us now was a wall full of dials and red buttons that lit up when something was not functioning properly. It could even show when someone was smoking in a cabin! This engine room was also Alberto's domain and now that we could hear each other speak, he tried to explain the mysteries of reconditioning the auxiliary engine, his current problem. When he started on changing the fuel injectors and crank house inspection, I lost concentration and wandered along the corridor to peer into an enormous freezer room where the meat, fish and dairy products were stored. Beside it was a smaller room just for ice cream and beyond that a long corridor filled along one side with a mountain of bagged potatoes. As I returned, Alberto was describing the engine-room logbook, which he had to read and adjust twice daily, at eleven-thirty in the morning and eleven-thirty at night. Warming to our interest, he said proudly, " I have been at sea for thirty-six years, the last eight years on this ship." He drew a diagram on some paper, showing the small island in the Philippines where his wife and four of their children lived. His eldest son was also at sea on another ship, and he saw his family only once a year. A shy, kind man, seldom seen by the passengers, Alberto's world is defined by this dim room of blinking lights and the millions of nuts and bolts he and his team lovingly tend every day.

It was strange to re-enter the lift again and find ourselves, a few moments later, emerging in the carpeted lobby on main deck. All at once, the floral arrangements, decorative table lamps and gleaming cabinets seemed ostentatious and unnecessary on board a real ship. On deck for some deep gulps of fresh air, I realised that the one sound I had missed for the last hour was the rush of the bow waves and the gentle hum of the engine, always present while we're at sea. I couldn't imagine the eerie experience of silent engines below decks. Was it only when the ship was in dry dock for repairs that every single piece of machinery is switched off? Sadly there were so many other new things to find out that I forgot to ask. Today the sea was calm and there was hardly a breeze to stir the parasols shading the sunbathers on deck. It was a real cruise brochure day, sunny and warm, and I resolved to make the most of it and join them. I would find a quiet place on the top deck (between the stacks) where the off-duty entertainment team would go for a rest between the many activities they organised all day long. They were not inclined to talk and just wanted a rest between sessions.

Sadly, as we eventually found out on a later cruise, the brochures were not always right. There are times when the weather is not quite so kind!

Water

It is easy to forget how important water is when one is surrounded by it most of the time. There is a desalination plant on board ship that provides most of the ship's fresh water. Other fresh water taken on at foreign ports is kept in a holding tank until it has been tested and cleared for general use. Most passengers drink bottled water in their cabins but in the restaurants, the water in our glasses comes from the ship's filtered supply. Perhaps due to the occasional problems reported in the press about the safety of water supplies on land, some passengers are suspicious about the quality of water on board. I suppose it does taste different. One evening an irate passenger, evidently suspicious of this provision, accosted us in the corridor. He wanted the medical centre opened so he could get a glass of water to help him swallow his pills. Perhaps he thought we had our own private supply? On another occasion, a sick passenger in one of the first class suites refused the bottle of water brought by the nurse to help combat her dehydration because she didn't want to pay for it. "Human beings are very contrary sometimes," I thought to myself.

The swimming pools are refilled daily with seawater, which is then heated to a comfortable temperature. I found them too warm for vigorous swimming but then they are not really large enough for more than a languorous splash around. Recreational water can cause problems, though. On one cruise the autopilot suddenly malfunctioned and the ship turned sharply. The water in the pool spilled over the decks and down into some of the passengers' cabins, which must have been a bit of a shock if you happened to be having an afternoon snooze. In choppy seas also, the swimming pool could suddenly become more of a challenge. The water whirls and splashes as you swim and it's like being in your own personal washing machine. The unwary, lunching at the poolside bar, may get a surprise soaking from an unlikely wave.

One morning, Leonie the nurse took me on her daily water tour. Carrying her smart blue plastic case we went first to the swimming pool deck to test the water in the Jacuzzis. The water there is even hotter than the swimming pools and if ever there are going to be bugs lurking, they will be found here. Inside the case was a neat collection of phials and bottles and a small machine like a rather bulky calculator that tested the pH of the water. Leonie collected a small sample in a bottle and mixed it with some pink liquid. Then she popped it in the machine and a decimal number appeared on the screen. The results were written down in a notepad neatly fastened to the lid of the case. Next, she took another sample and mixed it with a few drops of liquid from two other phials. This was a test for the level of chlorine and today it was too high. Next we tested the water in the drinking fountain at the outside bar and then went down in the lift to the galley. We checked where the galley crew washed their hands. They used a deep, stainless steel basin furnished with a large container of bactericidal soap and a roll of paper towel. Above the sink there was a printed message to 'Wash Your Hands.' The small potboy nearby grinned a welcome at us. Wearing bright yellow rubber gloves, he was immersed in soapy water up to his elbows and looked as if he needed a stool to reach the sink more comfortably. Nearby there was a loud crashing of crockery and cutlery, as the dishwashers were being endlessly filled and emptied by other galley staff. We went down again to the main galley on deck two in a small metal lift. The galley stretched ahead of us for what seemed to me to be the entire length of the ship. Gleaming counters of stainless steel were interspersed with tall racks for crockery. There were drawers and cupboards above the counters but everything was closed and tidy so I couldn't see what they contained. The sparkling, tiled floor looked clean enough to eat off. We tested the water in the taps above a long sink, where several people could work together. The chefs looked surprised to see me but smiled and greeted us. We moved on to the washing up room behind the crew mess and tested more water there. The crew mess was large and bright where the sun poured in through the portholes. Tables covered with cheerful blue and white plastic cloths lined one side and the centre of the room, and steam rose gently from the hot food counter on the other side. There was one large container of rice but I couldn't tell whether it was breakfast or lunch in the others or perhaps an amalgam of both. At nine-thirty in the morning the room was empty. We walked back through a long corridor and emerged opposite the medical centre.

Leonie filed her results on the daily forms, all of which showed the chlorine levels were too high. She will email these results to the bridge and also to the chief engineer, whose job it is to adjust the levels.

Within the next few days there were more watery

experiences. All new crew who have just joined ship must attend the Survival at Sea course. I didn't have to take part in this, because being labelled Supernumery, or Officer's family, I was neither crew nor passenger. Captain Trimble, the officer in charge of training, was a former Merchant Navy Captain. Word quickly went round when it was known that he was on board, for his powers of observation and attention to detail were legendary. With a booming voice, piercing blue eyes and beaky nose, I privately re-named him Captain Tremble because everyone seemed slightly nervous of him. His lectures were open to anyone and he was a good speaker, so one afternoon when the new crew candidates had gone off for a tea break, I went to the front of the theatre to have a look at all the articles kept in a life raft. Spread out on a table, it was hard to imagine how they could all possibly fit in. I picked up a heavy blow-up plastic pocket that turned out to be the baler, and a strange tool that automatically releases the raft and causes it to inflate. I counted three rubber bungs to block holes in the life raft, a patch repair kit, one knife and two oars. There was a quoit and line to throw to someone in the water, a hand pump and a mysterious box labelled McMurdoch's Aids to Marine Safety. There were parachute flares and hand flares that let off red or orange smoke, an emergency beacon and a radar transponder. I was relieved about this last one because it seemed the only thing that didn't rely on us being seen. There is an awful lot of sea out there. I found two black canes and wondered if they were for fishing or waving, a hand mirror called a heliograph, and some spare bulbs and batteries in a plastic case. Fishing tackle, seasick bags, and glucose tablets, along with tins of food and water were neatly lined up, next to scissors.

There was a whistle and a torch and several other odd-shaped parcels but, surprisingly, no tin opener. How were we supposed to open the tinned food? I listened to other people, whose curiosity had drawn them over to the table, discussing what they would take with them in the life raft. Their choices varied from brandy to the Bible, with the younger element yearning for face cream and a bar of soap. I smiled at this intimation of cleanliness over godliness and hoped it would never be put to the test.

At the end of the lecture we all went out to the swimming pool to watch the practical test. Armed with a camera, I found what I hoped was a splash-proof seat and sat down. For the next hour or so I was in charge of the "bleep". This was an electronic call device, which warned the Doc when he was needed. He would have to go to the nearest phone on board to answer the call. Putting this machine in a prominent position so I could hear it if it went off, I hoped it would stay silent. If not, a very wet doctor would confront the unsuspecting patient! The candidates had been told to dress warmly and wear tracksuits over swimwear with lifejackets on top. This clothing immediately caused problems for some, as four at a time, they leapt into the water. Some of the tracksuits ballooned up with water so that their occupants looked like Michelin men bobbing around, while other materials became transparent like cling film causing some sniggers around me, or else stretched to twice their normal size. Under a cascade of water from the fire hose to simulate heavy seas, the new crew practised rescuing potential drowning bodies and towed them to the side. There was a great deal of laughter, quickly quelled by the amount of chlorinated water swallowed. Captain Tremble, yelling commands from the side and with his white hair covered with a navy-blue bobble hat, kept leaping in and out of the water and was swift to punish any candidate who didn't seem to be taking the exercise seriously enough, by making them do it again. It was noticeable that he kept to the shallow end of the pool so that his arms, waving like windmills and wildly gesticulating signals to a hapless swimmer, were not impeded. It was not a large swimming pool, but quite large enough to intimidate crew who, like the Doc, had not experienced this kind of learning situation before.

Then came the second part of the exercise. When it was manoeuvred into the water, the inflatable life raft took up half the space in the pool and had a nasty habit of moving backwards just as someone stepped into it. Some missed altogether and the spectators cheered loudly. When the raft was full of heaving legs and plump bottoms, the Captain blew the whistle and they all had to jump out again. Learning how to tip the upturned life raft the right way up was even more difficult. Unless the timing was right, it was very easy to get stuck underneath and the rubber raft landed on several heads. Red-faced and spluttering, the victims emerged eventually only to be told to try again. Although my sides were aching with suppressed laughter, I felt sorry for the Doc who was not a keen swimmer at the best of times, and much prefers to paddle on the edge! In the end, he and everyone else achieved success and fortunately the last and most difficult exercise was saved for another day. It involved jumping off the side of the ship wearing a total immersion suit and would take place in Lanzerote where, hopefully, the sea would be warm. Now that really is going to be a baptism of fire or do I mean water?

Memorable People and Places

Cruises are known for tempting people to eat more than usual, and there are so many opportunities to test one's taste buds that it's hard to resist. One passenger, of Eastern European origin, owned many restaurants of his own so perhaps felt it was his duty to try out everything. We nicknamed him Uncle Bulgaria after a character in a long ago Children's TV programme, the Wombles. At mealtimes other passengers would watch in amazement as he arrived at the table with a plate piled high with a grand selection of the lunch buffet. Unable to speak English very well, he had no excuse to stop between mouthfuls and would eat his way through plateful after plateful. Already overweight, the rolls of fat surrounding his neck grew steadily and he began to look like a large round ball. At our next port of call, the European liaison officer gave him the usual shore-going instructions including the time to be back on board ship, all written in Spanish, his home language, especially for him.

As sailing time grew near it was realised that Uncle Bulgaria was not on board. The Captain delayed our departure but still he did not arrive. Unable to wait any longer the ship sailed without him. Half an hour later someone noticed a plume of spray from a small boat streaking towards us. The ship slowed and a pilot boat carrying Uncle Bulgaria drew alongside. Unfortunately by this time, many passengers were lining the ship's rails, cameras at the ready. Pretty soon it became obvious that Uncle Bulgaria was not going to be able to leap from the pilot boat into the ship like the agile pilots. We watched while he was encased in a large strait-jacket attached to ropes and a cheer went up as he was swung on board by four of the ship's stalwart deckhands. A little depressed after this incident, Uncle Bulgaria kept a low profile for a few days.

My favourite tour director worked alone in a small office near the reception counter. Patrick was a seriously efficient man whose whole life was based around his job of organising tours for passengers at the many ports of call. With no apparent home ties he lived for his work and was good at it. He knew exactly where to go, where not to go and how much to pay for taxis in any part of the world and I always consulted him to help organise our visits ashore. He was especially useful to us when the Doc only had an hour or two off because of work commitments. On an overnight stay we seldom left the ship in the evening because the nurses often liked the rare opportunity of going off together while we looked after the medical centre. This time however, we were free and Patrick invited us to join him and two of the ship's entertainers at a restaurant in St Petersburg. We leapt at the chance to see something of the city at night but getting to the restaurant was slightly alarming. Standing on the edge of the road outside the port, Patrick waved down two taxis. Our taxi had no springs in the back seat, which was covered with a hairy blanket. It also had no seatbelts and we bounced from side to side as we hurtled round roundabouts missing other cars by inches. Thankfully we made it safely to a quiet, dimly lit street, and were relieved to see Patrick and the others emerging from the other car behind us.

The restaurant was warm and welcoming. Seated at a large table in the centre of the room and surrounded by other diners, our meal commenced with vodka. Our fellow guests, a male dancer and his boyfriend, a musician on holiday from another cruise ship, were out to have a memorable evening and, out of sight of his colleagues and the passengers, the Doc was inclined to join in enthusiastically! There were several courses, at least five I seem to remember, and though strangely I don't recall what we ate for most of them I do know that different flavoured vodkas had to be swallowed in one gulp accompanied by raised glasses and a toast, preceding each. Our pronunciation of 'scholl', the Russian word for 'cheers', became more and more slurred as the hours passed. Not being a great drinker I was pleased to find that the vodka was quite palatable and in fact didn't really taste of anything much, that is until you swallowed it! After the meal a small group of musicians appeared and moved from table to table serenading the diners. Their music, lively and rousing at first, grew more nostalgic until finally, unable to ignore his Welsh roots any longer, our musical companion requested a song. His rendition of Mario Lanza's "Be My Love" brought a lump to my throat and wild applause from everyone. Of course, after that we had to spend another half hour singing a variety of patriotic songs from all our nations until the staff gently persuaded us all to pay up and leave. With one arm firmly linked to the Doc and the other to the Tour Director I stood on the pavement outside until the two younger men, deciding the night was still young, went off to find a nightclub. We reluctantly found another taxi and went back to the ship. The next day, having lost that lovely fuzzy feeling of the night before and with a slight headache, I hoped that the passengers had all been safely tucked up in bed and had not been watching our wobbly progress along the quay towards our floating home.

Going ashore in St Petersburg always required careful planning. On later cruises we found that the rules had been changed and everyone except the crew, had to have a visa to go ashore. It never seemed worthwhile applying for this when we were only here for two days but, without one, I would only be allowed ashore if I was on one of the ship's tours.

This time, joining forces with friends before the cruise, we planned to hire a private minivan with driver and guide. Sharing the expense made the trip comparable in price with a ship's tour but had the advantage of being in a small group of six able to choose our own itinerary. On the day, of course, the inevitable happened. Morning clinic was unusually busy and was followed by an unexpected crew drill. We all waited with bated breath. Would we be in time for our tour? Happily, just before eleven o'clock we were able to walk down the gangway and make our way through the Russian Customs' gates.

Elena, our guide, wore a brightly coloured skirt and a red blouse with a daring neckline. Her high heels teetered dangerously over the cobbles outside the Peter and Paul Fortress but we could not fault her explanation of the lives of the Russian aristocracy as we studied their tombs inside the cavernous cathedral. Actually, it was not their lives but their deaths that Elena elaborated upon in great detail. "The Romanovs are buried here with their symbol of the double-headed eagle," she announced with relish. Thousands of lives were lost in the building of the fortress itself and Peter the Great's son, Alexei, was the first of many to be tortured within its prison walls in 1718. After this rather gruesome piece of history we were led to a narrow corridor with chairs across the middle and invited to sit down. After a few minutes a group of monks arrived and began singing a Russian orthodox version of the Lords Prayer. With long pudding-basin hair cuts they looked like soberly gowned clones of the Beatles when young.

Outside, while Elena tried to gain control of her gypsy skirt billowing in the breeze, we jumped back into our spacious minivan to be transported to Peter's Cottage. This was the original cabin that Peter the Great had built for himself in May 1703 so that he could keep a close eye on the construction of the Peter and Paul Fortress nearby. A modern building had been built over and around the simple wooden hut to preserve it so that, despite being three hundred years old, it has not deteriorated. Built of rough-hewn pine logs, you could still see the white lines painted to resemble bricks on the outside. Inside, we had to wait a while for the curator who gave us a personal tour. As she spoke no English Elena had to translate. This was a bit confusing because we all wanted to peer in through the windows to see inside the three furnished rooms but didn't want to be impolite and ignore the voluble flow of Russian on our left and the following English on our right!

Our final visit to the Alexander Pushkin Apartments was nearly abandoned because we had lost time in the terrible traffic jams in the city. The famous poet leased this apartment for his wife, her two sisters and their four children during the last year of his life in 1836. The eleven rooms on the second floor were interesting as a way of looking at an affluent family apartment, though apparently Pushkin, who was in ill health, couldn't always keep up with the rent. One of the few of his personal effects on show in the study was a clock that had been stopped, according to Russian tradition, at the moment of his death and stands frozen, at 2.45 pm. When we had returned to the ship we decided that death and the 'double-headed eagle', had been the macabre theme of the day and that Elena had really enjoyed filling in all the gruesome details.

During the time of Catherine the Great, the staterooms of the Winter Palace were opened for evening receptions. She called these rooms her 'Hermitage', a place where she could escape from the trials of state affairs. Catherine would invite clever, talented friends to join her and amuse her with interesting conversation. In return, she would show them the latest additions to her growing art collection while listening to a distinctive, musical recital.

That evening, after clinic, we ate a hasty meal and joined the ship's tour by coach to the Hermitage that was closed to the general public. We felt privileged to be able to walk through the galleries without the crowds of daytime sightseers. It was so much easier to appreciate the beauty of the golden ceilings, curved staircases and marble pillars and get close to some of the priceless paintings and sculptures. At one point my eyes fell on the room monitor, a blank-faced woman of late middle age sitting in one corner. This army of Russian women, one in every room, always seemed to wear nondescript clothes and ankle socks as if they did not want to be noticed. My efforts to make them return my smile were never successful.

Afterwards we followed our guide up a long flight of stairs where waiters with trays of glasses awaited us. Champagne, fizzing gently, was a great prelude to a concert in the Skylight Italian Hall. As the Doc only allowed himself a small sip, I cheerfully consumed the rest of his as well as my own. Members of the State Symphony Orchestra were seated in a semi-circle in the centre of the smaller hall and played music by Mozart just for us. I gazed upwards at ornate blue and gold patterns decorating the upper walls as rays of late evening sunlight drifted in through the enormous glass skylight, illuminating the group of musicians and the white, marble sculptures beyond them. Afterwards, still heady with the effects of my refreshments, and not wanting the evening to end, I lingered at the base of a huge, blue vase made of lapis lazuli and imagined that full of champagne too!

Norway and Iceland

As our cruise line originated in Norway I always feel that this country is its spiritual home. On four of the five visits we made to Bergen, the second largest city in Norway and home of the composer Edward Grieg, we had days of fine sunny weather in a city notorious for its rainfall. But I looked forward to the Norwegian fjords, which were always springing surprises on us, providing experiences that were different and sometimes quite challenging. The ship glides smoothly along the calm depths of the fjords that reflect the mountains on either side until we come to one of the small towns and settlements that are huddled together along the banks, often at the end of a fjord. Usually passengers are tendered ashore and sometimes while they're away the ship goes to the other end of the fjord and waits to collect her sightseeing guests.

On this day, we anchored early at Hellesylt, a small village on the western arm of Geiranger fjord and I went ashore for a long hike through the mountains. A coach took us to the start of the walk at Vollseter Farm, along a stony track with a gradual incline. It was easy walking at a comfortable pace with plenty of photo stops but difficult to imagine that before roads were built this was once the only highway for people to travel over the mountains. We passed three lakes that mirrored the mountains above them so perfectly that I couldn't tell which was the reflection in my viewfinder. Waterfalls tumbled from a great height like streaks of long white hair, sometimes combining with others to form a powerful, frothy mass of white water at the bottom. There were sheep and cows wearing bells, some reluctant to get off the path so that we had to drive them in front until the path was wide enough to scurry past. We stopped at a 'seter', a summer home built of wood with a grass roof, and had homemade soup and a bread roll, sitting at solid picnic tables. It felt good to eat a picnic on top of a mountain in the fresh air. The toilets were also wooden huts on stilts with a long drop and no water. Seters were formerly used as summer homes for farmers living with their animals for summer pasturing. Now they have fallen out of use but are gradually being restored as holiday homes for families. Our coach was waiting at the bottom of the mountain beside Lake Stryn and after coffee and cakes at a local café we drove to Mount Dalsnibba, a harrowing five kilometres up a gravel road with no safety barriers. Admiring the views from the summit, I looked down to where the ship lay at anchor in Geirangerfjord below, a tiny toy boat, with a picture frame reflection of the snow-covered mountains behind us.

Olden is another picturesque village along Norffjord in western Norway. The Briksdal Glacier is not far away and we had planned our own outing to climb it. Not all of it, just a small section at the beginning. I was not sure what to wear so put on layers of clothes that could be peeled off if necessary and strong walking shoes with two pairs of socks. On deck it was hot and sunny and I looked out of place with the sunbathers stretched out in swimwear. Hoping it wouldn't get too hot, I hurried away to join the passengers going ashore. We had organised a taxi to take us to the start of the climb.

The base of the glacier was problematic in places. After walking over a wide gravelled area, we reached a bank of large pebbles and rubble that had to be crossed carefully. This is known as scree and has gradually travelled down the mountain over time. My strong shoes seemed a good idea now as it was quite unpleasant to walk on and the air was much colder in the shadow of the glacier. The ice, when we reached it, was a dirty grey colour with black streaks in it. I felt a pang of disappointment but the guide assured us that higher up it would look better. I was also feeling a little nervous. I had never done any climbing and had no idea what to expect. There were ten of us and we clustered round Klaus, the Norwegian guide, as he explained how to put on our crampons.

We were given an ice axe and a heavy belt by which we would be attached to him with a rope in awkward places. By then I was seriously wishing I was back on deck with the sun worshippers, but it was too late for regrets and we were soon moving off. We walked slowly, putting one foot at a time into the ice and feeling the grip of the spikes. Once I got used to them I found it quite comforting. It was like being a fly on a wall with sticky feet. As I gained confidence I tried to turn round quickly to talk to someone behind me and nearly fell flat on my face. I turned but my feet didn't!

Gradually we climbed higher and the ice mountain got steeper. We left the chattering tourists behind at ground level and it was so quiet we could all hear the heavy breathing and occasional grunts from the person behind us. Soon we were concentrating so hard that there wasn't time or breath to talk. At last we reached steps cut in the ice. Klaus went up first and I watched how he used his ice axe as an extra support to climb. He threw down a rope and the next person in line fixed it to the big clip on his belt. Soon it was my turn and I ascended slowly, glad of the rope and hoping I wouldn't slip. Perhaps because I'm left-handed, I was not very good with the axe and found it more of a hindrance than a help. At the top we stood in a line, flushed with the effort but inwardly exhilarated. The muscles in my legs and arms were trembling and I wondered if anyone else was feeling the same. There was still some way to go. Ahead of us lay a steady climb on snow-covered ice that was pristine white. Our path had markers, placed earlier in the day by the guides to prevent anyone plunging into a hole, so we could relax a little now and take in the scenery.

The sky was an intense shade of blue and the ice too reflected a bluish hue with deeper shades of green and purple in places. In one direction, as far as the eye could see there was nothing else but these two colours. Then we turned to listen to Klaus as he told us about crevices. In the distance there was a roaring noise. "Avalanche," he said. "Talk quietly. Voices can start them off." We had more steps to climb before we reached our summit, not the real one but it was as far as we could safely go. We could see the glacier properly now between the mountains, a long white ribbon reaching to the skyline. Below us the cars and coaches sprawled along the valley floor and we whispered among ourselves after Klaus' warning. After the clicking of cameras had ceased, we began the descent that seemed to take longer, because some of us were wary of going backwards down the ice steps. Klaus and another man abseilled down but the rest of us took our time.

At the bottom, we started the hike back to Briksdal village, leaving our crampons and other equipment for the next group. Although it had seemed to be an eternity, the whole experience had only taken a couple of hours. As I glanced back to take a last look, I found it difficult to believe I had really climbed a glacier (well, at least part of one), but I do have the photographs to prove it.

Iceland was another country that I knew little about before our cruise there in 2004. I spent several hours on deck sheltering from the cold wind and dodging frequent icy showers just watching the water, gazing at the horizon and remembering my father's tales about this part of the world. All ready to retire from the navy in 1939, just before the second World War, he had found himself re-engaged and his ship, HMS Norfolk, attached to the Home Fleet, which was deployed on Northern Patrol, in the Denmark Straits, between Iceland, Greenland and the Shetlands. He had described it as "a cold wearisome job. During the winter you had practically one long, long night." He had blamed the poor light on the deterioration of his eyesight and when being fitted with glasses had to have them specially made to go under a gas mask. I still have those glasses in their thin metal case at home.

I had always imagined Iceland to be a country of permanent snow and ice, and we had passed a great deal of scattered ice by the time we reached our berth with the help of the ice pilot. It was a surprise to find the capital, Reykjavik, bathed in summer sunshine. The word Reykjavik means 'Smoky Bay' and the city is so named because of the steam rising from its many geothermal features. Geothermal heat and strong winds provide power for the whole city.

As we were only here for one day we had to be pretty selective about our sightseeing. The Doc was limited to a few hours ashore so plumped for a trip to the Blue Lagoon, which sounded intriguing. It's not really a lagoon at all but a large pool of effluent from the local Svartsengi power plant about 50kms from Reykjavik. Leaving the city, we drove past a huge glass dome nicknamed 'The Pearl' that sat on top of hot water storage tanks. On either side of the road were strangely shaped lava fields. The guidebook I was reading as we bumped along on the bus, described the water as having deposits of silica mud together with an organic soup of dead algae, which were supposed to be good for skin complaints. I resolved not to swallow any!

The pool, when we arrived, was wreathed in swirling clouds of steam hiding the water. Standing on the edge in my swimsuit newly purchased from the ship's boutique, it looked a peculiar grey colour and was surrounded by a high lava wall. The adjacent power plant was hidden from view except for occasional gaps in the steam. The water was a balmy 37-39 degrees, too hot to swim energetically but wonderful to lounge in. I moved cautiously from one area to another because the temperature changed and it became suddenly hotter in places. All around the pool there were platforms with ceramic basins filled with mud that people were smearing on their faces. We copied them and laughed at each other with our ghostly white masks. Washing it off again proved difficult but I was feeling so indolent and relaxed that I completely forgot about the decayed algae. Anyway, whatever was in the mud left our skins feeling soft and clean all the way back to the ship and well into the evening, after we sailed away through the icebergs en-route to Cape Farewell and Greenland.

The Storm

Rumours spread like wildfire around Black Prince, the smallest cruise ship of the fleet. We were on the homeward section of a cruise to the Mediterranean. The weather forecast, always a source of interest, was not good. By five o'clock just before we left Lisbon, there was a stiff breeze blowing. The damp white folds of fog that enabled us to slip beneath the Bridge over the Tagus in muffled secrecy that morning had gone. On our return journey we enjoyed a clear view of the bridge and the awe-inspiring Christ statue guarding it as we sailed towards a brilliant pink and yellow sunset.

Over dinner in the restaurant an exaggerated forecast emerged. Our companions suspected we were heading for a force ten gale. We listened patiently to tales of other storm-bound cruises, but in the comfort of the dining room, warmed by a glass or two of red wine, the mood was one of excitement rather than alarm. Some people ate as though it was their last supper, while other, wiser passengers are more cautious. Some soup and a light main course will see them through the night. As we left the shelter of the estuary, the ship began to dance an uncomfortable jig and by eleven o'clock most passengers retired for the night replete with seasickness tablets, if not a good meal. Already it was difficult to walk normally and we clung to the rails and banisters and slid along the walls of the corridor towards our cabins laughing and joking at our lack of control. "Oh, help," shrieked a plump lady in front of us as a sudden jolt sent her pitching forward. She looked delighted as the Doc offered her a helpful arm. There's nothing like a man in uniform to calm things down!

The long night was terrible. The ship took on a creaking, groaning life of it's own. Every piece of furniture had a song to sing. In my bunk, I leant on one elbow and tried to identify the violent tapping just above my head. No it was not above my head, it was from the desk beside me. I got up and fretfully rearranged the contents but the problem was not solved. I slept but only fitfully as the bed rose and fell in rhythm with the contents of my stomach and the cabin noises increased in intensity. Abandoning sleep and my own bunk (no double bed in this ship!), I crept across the cabin to squeeze in between my sleeping husband and the wall. This, of course, woke him and then neither of us could sleep.

By morning, measurable only by our watches because we had an inside cabin with no porthole, it was almost impossible to stay upright. I stayed in bed because it required too much effort to get up, but work had to go on, so the Doc struggled into uniform and disappeared to the Officers' mess for breakfast telling me forcefully to stay where I was. At nine o'clock, awoken from an uneasy doze by the tannoy system, the Captain informed us, unnecessarily, that we were in the midst of a severe storm. "Stay in your cabins and avoid moving about," was his advice, but I wanted to see the thirty-metre high waves he had just reported to be breaking over the ship and besides, I'm crew's wife, not really a passenger at all! Trying to avoid the swinging wardrobe doors that burst open at every opportunity, I spread my clothes on the floor and dressed sitting down.

The journey along the corridor and up two flights of stairs required cunning and stamina. Wait for a roll to complete itself, and you were propelled onwards, but hesitate and you are flung backwards in the wrong direction. I joined a few brave souls in the lounge and gazed in awe at the waves. They were higher than the ship, grey-green and mean as they hunted us down. Stuck in a trough we paused as if suspended, until the wave hit the side and a shudder ran through the whole ship. From somewhere there was the sound of breaking glass. The hum of the tannoy again alerted us to a new message from the bridge. "There is a problem with the engines. It is necessary to turn them off and as a consequence the ship will roll heavily. Stay in your cabins or sit on the floor." What had really been an exciting event was beginning to turn into something more sinister. Another wave hit the side of the ship and there was a loud bang. In the lounge beneath the balcony where we were sitting, all the cups and saucers were thrown on the floor to smash and mingle with the musical instruments that had slid off the stage. Several people lay sprawled on the carpet amidst the mess. Although they didn't appear to be injured, and, afraid to use the lift, I clung and half-slid down the stair rail and went to warn the medical team that they might have a casualty, but the hospital was empty.

In our cabin everything had fallen out of the wardrobes. Hastily, I pushed it all back in and tied the handles together with a dressing-gown cord. Then I put bottles of shampoo and makeup in the sink, wrapped in a towel to stop them clattering around. There was just time to throw some more loose articles into the wastepaper bin, before the ship started to roll. There was nothing to do but lie flat on the bed, duvet rolled beneath my head, feet braced against the headboard. The stool slid gently forward and back, followed by books, shoes, and anything else that was not tied down. There were dreadful crashing noises overhead and I was suddenly afraid. I wished the Doc was there and we could be together. The Norwegian Captain's voice boomed out again. "There is a small fire in one of the lounges, but do not worry because everything is under control." His richly accented English was comforting but alone in the cabin I couldn't help feeling anxious. Should I stay here or go and find someone, anyone, to keep me company? Deciding on some action to stop my wimpish panic, I managed with great difficulty to get our two life jackets out of the wardrobe and fumbled for my warm fleece. I pushed a wool scarf and some socks into the pockets then lay down again. Time seemed to go very slowly. It was difficult to read and the TV screen showed only black and white dots and dashes. I was pleased when the Doc put his head round the door to check on me before rushing off again to suture a cut on someone's hand. I passed the next few hours somehow alternatively dozing and attempting to read while listening to the creaks and rattles around the cabin. Despite my curiosity about things happening outside, notified by the occasional loud voice in the corridor, it seemed wiser to stay where I was.

Later that day, when the wind had moderated and the engines were going again, the passengers emerged from their cabins to stare at the shambles. The boutique was in ruins; pictures and wall displays were wrecked and shattered china lay everywhere. I made myself useful in the hospital, and crawled around the floor collecting syringes, pills and plastic containers of all shapes and sizes, returning them to the desk to be sorted out by the nurses. A potted plant and its soil mingled with books, papers and patients' notes that would have to be recycled and re-typed later in the day.

The galley had lost hundreds of plates and had no electricity for the time being so there was no hot food. As most of us had had no breakfast, the trays of sandwiches that came around later were welcomed, in the camping-out atmosphere on board. We sat on a carpet in the biggest lounge and demolished them from paper plates, the chairs having been roped off in a corner. Passengers exchanged horror stories of their own about the disintegration of their cabins. Some of them on the upper decks told us with great relish that they were thrown out of their bunks but fortunately didn't appear to be injured. There was nothing else to do but sit and gossip, since the day's activities had been suspended, while all around us, the pale-faced crew-members went quietly about their work and cleared up the mess. The ship still shuddered and lurched at unexpected moments but the worst was over. The Captain reported that we had survived rolls of thirty-two degrees, a wind off the top of the Beaufort scale and thirty-eight metre high waves. As the ship continued on its voyage home a feeling of camaraderie developed on board. Marjorie and Tom, who sat with me in the lounge and watched the waves at the height of the storm, became real friends and we exchanged addresses and hoped to meet again on a calmer sea. Together with the crew we came through an experience we all hoped would not happen again, but it was a timely reminder that cruising is not always a 'blue sky and gentle breezes' holiday.

Emailing Fidel

One of our cruises in the Caribbean went to Cuba and three of our table companions on this trip were an American couple travelling with their friend Claudette, who was French and lived in Belgium. Together with a lone Scotsman travelling solo, we made a lively group. Every evening at dinner, the lean American, Walter, asked us if we had had a good day. His pretty wife, Deidre, white hair exquisitely groomed, traced a delicate pattern with a blood-red finger nail on the table cloth and listened while he told us all about his day. She interrupted occasionally to correct him, but her gentle sense of humour robbed her remarks of any criticism. Their French companion, Claudette, had a quick wit and an ability to switch from French to Spanish to English which added spice to the conversation. The three had met years ago and now always cruised together. I was fascinated by the amazing collection of rings Claudette wore. Sometimes I wondered how she could lift her fork with the weight of them. I found myself surreptitiously staring but she caught me looking and laughed, explaining that rings were her little weakness. Seldom meeting during the day, we enjoyed sharing a meal in the evenings and comparing notes on the Caribbean islands so far visited and which we preferred.

We were all looking forward to Cuba. Walter had

been there while working for the American government many years before, but he was reticent about his former occupation saying only that it was involved with refugees. I was intrigued and curious because of Walter's obsession with the island. He confided that in more recent years he had written to Fidel Castro asking if he could bring his wife to Havana to celebrate their wedding anniversary. He produced a crumpled envelope from the pocket of his dinner jacket. The letter still inside, already fifteen years old, was from the Cuban Minister of Tourism, giving them permission to enter the country. Sadly, Deidre had been too afraid to come and she was still only willing to go ashore as long as Jim carried this faded token of acceptance with him. Because of the United States embargo at that time, Americans could normally only enter the country from cruise ships and could not spend any dollars there. Going to Cuba had become a kind of pilgrimage for Walter and I'm sure that the rest of the cruise did not matter to him.

Claudette was excited because she loved Cuban music and wanted to go to the famous show at the Tropicana Hotel. We were pleased when they invited us to join them for the evening but we had to warn them that a doctor's life is unpredictable and that plans might have to be changed at the last minute if someone became ill. The arrangements for the evening were in Walter's hands. Deidre did not want to go by coach with an organised tour. It would be far too crowded and we wouldn't get good seats. She had reached the stage in life where comfort came before economy. While fully agreeing with this in theory we privately both hoped it wouldn't be too expensive and I made a mental note to use the ship's banking facilities and withdraw more dollars.

Mysterious hints about contacts made me even more curious. Walter intimated that he knew someone who could get tickets for us and Claudette offered to pay for them initially. At dinner that evening Walter was preoccupied and a little morose and it was a relief when Claudette caused a diversion by ordering red wine and a bucket of ice to chill it. I didn't tell her that at home we usually stand our red wine by the boiler to warm it and thought you only chilled white wine.

Cuba is the largest island in the Caribbean. On the morning of our arrival I went up on deck early and perched on the edge of a canvas seat, clutching a cup of tea and a croissant as the ship moved along the waterfront towards the port in the centre of the old town of Havana. Behind me, the sky deepened into a deep pink as the sun rose, flushing the grey walls of a fort with benevolent colour. A long line of skyscrapers was silhouetted against a purple haze of pollution, and in front of them statues and church towers jostled with apartment blocks shuddering with age and decrepitude.

Standing on the balcony of the Customs building, shivering in the early morning air, were a group of scantily clad Cuban dancers waiting beside shrouded musical instruments to welcome us ashore. Sorting out customs formalities meant that they had a long, chilly wait. Then, because I was escorting a passenger tour that morning, I hurriedly left my perch to collect hat and sunglasses from our cabin. In the doorway I met the Doc who announced with some incredulity the latest report from Walter.

"He's emailed Fidel!"

"Fidel who?" I asked, and then burst into laughter. I wanted to know more but didn't have time to discuss the situation. Clutching my shore pass card, first aid bag and belongings I hurried to the gangway.

The faded graffiti pictures of Che Guevara still showed through later coats of paint on the building next to Revolution Square, but on a quiet early morning, it was difficult to imagine its awesome space full of chanting revolutionary workers. The coach swept past dilapidated facades of old colonial Spanish buildings, like skeletons from a long gone past, when Havana was a rich and beautiful city. Now, collapsing with age and neglect, they stood forlornly crisscrossed with scaffolding, paid for with money from UNESCO. I asked the guide where President Castro lived but she said that nobody knew. He has many houses in Havana and moves from one to another for security reasons. I couldn't begin to guess what it must be like to live such a cat and mouse life and wondered if Walter's email would ever get to him.

This local tour of the capital included some walking through crowded streets and required sharper eyes than usual to make sure no-one got lost, as we wandered from the picturesque cathedral square into a busy craft market. The guide's broken English needed some translation too at times so I didn't have much time to think about our plans for the evening.

Later that afternoon, making the most of two hours of freedom, the Doc and I went trotting through the town in a horse-drawn carriage. I felt vulnerable and exposed, not only because we were in the middle of the traffic but also because of our comparative wealth. How different we looked with our cameras and casual cruise wear. This wasn't a smart part of Havana and, all around, vehicles of ancient vintage drove past with belching exhausts and ear-splitting engines, but the blinkered horse seemed oblivious of the uproar. There were cars I recognised from old movies but had never seen, many of them lovingly polished despite battered, rusting exteriors. People in jumble sale clothes thronged the sidewalks or hung carelessly over balconies on which their possessions were piled in filthy confusion. We jolted along beside antique wooden trucks on the railway line and were overtaken by long pink buses with two carriages joined in the centre with accordion-like pleating. Sky blue Skodas hurtled past with screeching brakes while we overtook wiry men on bicycles pedalling furiously and towing single-seater carts behind. The backs of my legs stuck to the cracked leather seat as the heat intensified. Intent on establishing the cost of our fare, we had not thought to inspect the horse but the carriage itself was clearly past its best. I hoped it, or the animal, wouldn't collapse beneath us. Afterwards we sat in the shade of giant palms in buckets, listening to live Salsa music and drinking cold beer. We needed to pause awhile to absorb the vitality of this lovely, crumbling city. In the market I bought a collection of musical instruments made out of gourds and bamboo. They cost so little it seemed like stealing. I paid more for a small clay statue of Castro but couldn't resist buying it for Walter as a souvenir.

It was a shock to return to the gilded opulence of the ship. There was a note lying on the carpet beneath our cabin door. Everything for the evening was arranged. At seven-thirty while the Doc was finishing evening clinic I went to the reception lounge where we were to meet. Too excited to sit, I wandered up and down hoping and praying there wouldn't be a last minute medical emergency. Once off the ship we would be incognito and free. At last we reached the quay without mishap, though the customs officers looked slightly menacing as they inspected our passports yet again. Being used to European cities being lit up at night I was surprised by the lack of street lighting in the town, but despite this, groups of people laughed and chatted on dim corners or sat in rows along walls and steps lining the streets as we sped by in our air-conditioned people-carrier. Ushered to a table in front of the stage, laden with bottles of rum in buckets of ice and surrounded by cans of Coca-Cola, I was glad I had eaten an early but substantial dinner on board.

A large stage extended downwards in front of us, and as the orchestra began to play, it surged with wave after wave of dancers, dazzling in silver and white gowns. The throbbing beat of the music set my feet tapping and the changing colours reflected an eerie green glow on our upturned faces. It was difficult to know where to look next as row upon row of moving figures descended, filling the stage with rippling bands of colour. On either side high above our heads, there were more dancers on platforms, whose bright feathers and sequinned finery reminded me of strange exotic birds swaying in the branches of trees.

We watched spellbound, as the music softened to a seductive rumba, mesmerised by the lithe sensual movements of their bodies. Glancing sideways I caught Claudette's eye and smiled. I could tell that like me, she would love to have been one of those women, looking for just a few brief moments as if they owned the world. The finale, two hours later, when our tall glasses had only melting ice left in them, became a festive celebration. Invited by the dancers, some of the audience, limbs and inhibitions loosened with the aid of rum and coke, joined in. Others like us, who either felt too embarrassed to attempt the sinuous movements, or couldn't find a space, sang and clapped in time to the music. When it was finished, the lights dimmed and looking skywards I could see the moon and stars between the trees. The magical evening was over and it was time to go back to our floating home.

Dancing on deck in the warm night air and dipping into the midnight buffet was the perfect way to wind down. Our companions were leaving the next day to fly home to Florida so we gave Walter our farewell gift amidst much laughter. Tentatively I asked, "How did you get the tickets, Walter? Did you really email … er… him?" There was a pause.

"Well, it's a long story and I'd kinda like to go to bed now" he replied giving me a slow wink.

"Maybe, next time we meet, I'll tell ya all about it".

Emergencies

The Doc's essential needs while packing for a cruise are his medical bag and the British National Formulary book. These small items together with the well-equipped hospital on board see him through most kinds of medical emergency. I really only have two apart from my beloved kettle: a laptop computer and small travelling hairdryer.

While passengers are happily relaxing on board or sleeping in their beds, a code call on the loudspeakers instantly alerts the crew to an emergency and they swing into action. There are special and specific code names for emergencies, one for a fire, one for a bomb on board, one for a man overboard, an oil spillage and another for medical emergencies.

Passengers are always shielded from things that go wrong on board ship and sometimes are not even aware that an emergency is real. They get accustomed to regular crew practice drills, though many of these take place when the ship is in port and most people are ashore. On one long and memorable sea day the dreaded code for fire was broadcast just as we were enjoying an after lunch nap in our cabin. Instantly the Doc shook himself awake, collected the minimum items of uniform and shoes and joined the medical team assembled outside the medical centre. I put the kettle on to make some tea, my usual response to any feelings of mild panic I might have.

The medical team consisted of a doctor, two nurses and four stalwart crewmen who each have a role to play. While waiting for instructions from the bridge, they collect and check the stretchers, oxygen and other medical paraphernalia. Meanwhile, somewhere else on the ship the fire team assembled and was quickly sent to fight a small fire that had broken out near the engine room. It was a very hot day and many of the passengers were on deck sunbathing. They soon got used to seeing teams of men in full fire fighting gear disappearing into a door and later reappearing to be replaced by others, but only the most observant suspected this event was not a practice drill.

Down below the fire was persistent and there was a great deal of smoke. Working in such a confined space is difficult and painstakingly slow, as the area must be kept closed to prevent air entering and causing flames to flare up. Meanwhile in the medical centre the crew had long since given up looking alert and sat or sprawled on the carpet, their stretchers and oxygen cylinder pushed to one side. I joined them and suggested refreshments. The nurses were interested but reluctantly refused in case they were suddenly called away.

We listened anxiously to the discussions going forward and back between the bridge and the engine room on the crackling walky-talky phone held by Mary, the nurse. Because she kept turning the sound down when any passengers walked by, I missed bits and got a very disjointed picture of what was actually going on.

At last, the long afternoon came to an end and we were told all was safe and the fire was out. The medical team dispersed and had to rush back to complete jobs that were supposed to have been done earlier. The fire teams were exhausted but unharmed and no lasting damage prevented our continued journey across the ocean. That night before we went to sleep, I checked that all my clothes and items necessary for a quick exit from the room were easily available, for both of us!

The code everyone dreads is the one warning of a bomb on board. This is because all crew are involved and the drills can take place at any time. They are often just when we arrive in port and we sympathise with crew who were looking forward to going ashore for a few hours because all leave is immediately cancelled. On this occasion I was sitting in the library when I heard the alert. The crew came in and began to search in an orderly manner but I noticed they didn't look behind the long curtains at one of the windows. Just out of curiosity I waited until they had left the room and went to lift the curtain. Sure enough there was a small metal box placed on a ledge. Quickly I ran to find them and got a grateful "thank you Mrs Doc" from a relieved stewardess. Sadly, by the time they had been debriefed and released by the First Officer, it was hardly worth getting changed to go ashore and that phone call home usually made from the port terminal would have to wait for the next destination.

When the threat is perceived as real, however, there is no time for complacency. One time the ship received a satellite phone call saying that there was a bomb on board and the person calling gave enough clues to prove he should be taken seriously. We were in port, so in theory someone could have come aboard and planted a device. All other duties were suspended while the ship was searched but nothing was found. There was a slightly uneasy atmosphere on board that evening, undetected by the passengers, we hoped. Later, the Doc was told that it had been a hoax phone call from a disgruntled former crewmember.

Medical emergencies often happen in the middle of the night and this time it's the Doc who gets the phone call. The code sign is not activated then because it would wake everyone up. Our cabins have a bedside phone and the bleep machine is always with the Doc when he is on call. That's most of the time while we are on board because there is only one doctor on the short cruises. There are two doctors on transatlantic cruises and on the longer world cruises. The bleep is the size of a small mobile phone and fits in a pocket. When it goes off a small display window shows a number to ring. The Doc was used to waking quickly and after years of similar nocturnal interruptions I should be able to turn over and go back to sleep but somehow on board ship it's different. Sometimes I lay awake for a while listening to the drone of the engines or, if the sea was rough, listening to the waves crashing against the side. Our cabin on Black Watch was right up in the bows and when it was stormy, the creaks, bangs and tapping noises made me think I was in an old wooden sailing ship. Normally I found this quite romantic, but not the noises coming from behind the bed. The crew restroom was directly behind the wall and ghastly sounds from violent foreign movies on their TV kept the night shift workers and us awake during our mutual rest periods. Occasionally the Doc marched in there in his pyjamas and shouted at them to turn down the sound. For a few nights after that all was quiet until they forgot it was the middle of the night and the noise crept up again.

One night we were woken by a call from the Bridge. A crew member was seriously ill and as the night wore on it became obvious there were no easy options for his treatment. There are no anaesthetic or X-ray facilities on board and he needed an operation. Even at its highest speed it would take too long for the ship to divert to the nearest land so the decision was made to airlift him off the ship by helicopter. By now it was nearly dawn and the hospital lights were ablaze as I crept past to climb the eight flights of stairs to the top deck to wait for its arrival. The fire crew were already running safety hoses around the swimming pool area and checking that everything was ready. There was nobody else around at this early hour and I unpacked one of the sun beds from the stack to give myself somewhere to sit and wait.

At 5.45am I heard the drone of the helicopter that soon could be seen approaching in the grey, dawn light. The ship slowed down and a paramedic was lowered on a gently swaying rope, followed a few minutes later by another man with a stretcher. They conferred with the Doc and all disappeared below deck. Fifteen minutes later the team arrived with the patient on the stretcher. The rotor blades created a strong wind that made waves on the swimming pool and formed a fine spray of water to drench the medical team as the ropes were attached to the stretcher. The patient, as cocooned and firmly strapped as a mummy, was hoisted upwards turning slightly in the breeze, until strong arms pulled him aboard. I couldn't help hoping his eyes were shut and that he was fast asleep. The paramedics followed when the rope was lowered again and I took my last photo of their airborne wave as the helicopter turned and flew east towards the nearest land. I stayed alone and watched the sky go yellow with the sunrise, then went below for yet another cup of tea. The next morning the Doc waved a piece of paper at me as I walked past the Medical Centre. "Email from the hospital, operation successful," he said with a tired smile.

Having been a doctor's wife for many years, I'm used to people being taken ill at odd times and in inconvenient circumstances. It's the reaction to these that's important, sometimes being the one thing that can save someone's life. On one formal evening, my friend Joy and I went to the Captain's cocktail party so that she could have her photo taken with the Captain. Everyone was dressed in their glittery best. I wore my sparkling sweater, long black Laura Ashley skirt and a patterned jacket I had picked up for five pounds in a charity shop earlier in the year.

Afterwards, following a long and satisfying dinner, we decided to finish the evening in style and went to the show, leaving the Doc cabin-visiting to sort someone's medication problems. For that evening's entertainment there was a talented player of musical instruments, who played well and sang. Unfortunately his violin and mandolin didn't seem to be tuned properly with the orchestra, or else the amplification was not quite right so the sound was a bit peculiar. Following him came Andrew, my favourite singer, and we settled down to enjoy his songs from the shows.

Suddenly I noticed a slight commotion at the back of the theatre, so curious to see what was going on I left my seat and went to have a look. The waiters were circling around someone on the floor who appeared to be unconscious but it was dark and difficult to see. The only light came from one of the small torches used by the waiters when they served drinks. The Doc was nowhere to be seen but had apparently been summoned to the phone elsewhere. Someone had called for a code alpha (the emergency medical code) but the young officer on the bridge panicked and pressed the bell to abandon ship! This moment had unseen repercussions. On the crew deck, off duty crew, asleep in their beds, came out of their cabins with lifejackets and wandered round waiting for instructions. The Saga tour escort ladies, also in bed, became flustered. “I’m not going in my nightie,” one said to the other. The tour Director came out of his cabin thinking there was a fire. Meanwhile on stage, Andrew was bravely continuing to ‘Climb Every Mountain’ through the noise of the alarm bell and the increasing murmur at the back of the room. I hoped he would keep singing until the patient had been taken down to the hospital but there did seem to be a longer than usual delay. Finally a nurse who had also been fast asleep in bed, rushed in with the stretcher party, her hair sticking up on top of her head, and sternly gave orders to take the stretcher feet first. Officers came from all directions to peer into the darkness but it did not seem to occur to anyone to turn up the lights. Afterwards it all seemed very funny, but at the time it was a rather confusing interlude to say the least. The passenger recovered quickly from a simple fainting attack but I couldn’t help wondering how we would have managed had it been a real evacuation role call. Perhaps we should sometimes have emergency drills at night? Everything looks different in the dark.

Of course, things don’t always turn out so well. All cruise ships have a mortuary, usually compact and discreetly tucked away. On one ship it consisted of a refrigerated drawer just inside the entrance to the medical centre. Some crew are superstitious and prefer to avoid the room when there is a body ‘in situ.’ An Asian nurse in training at that time, whose cabin was attached to the clinic, was so disturbed that she refused to sleep in it and disappeared. It took some time to find her hiding place and persuade her to come out.

The Doc also caused a commotion late one evening

when he decided to take a bath in the medical centre. He made sure the coast was clear and, having locked himself in, he switched off all the lights except the bathroom one and popped in for a good soak. Unfortunately the crew member cleaning the surgery that night was late and while wielding her mop was horrified to see a ghostly naked figure wrapped in white emerge from the gloom. She ran shrieking to find her friends and the Doc hastily shot back to our cabin clutching his towel. It took him some while to live that one down.

Perhaps things were easier when bodies could be buried at sea. One evening a retired Merchant Naval officer friend dining with us mesmerised the entire table with a harrowing tale. One of his passengers had sadly died and his coffin was duly assembled on deck and covered with a blanket, the plan being to take it ashore at the next port of call for burial. Unfortunately, due to inclement weather, the ship wasn't able to get into port. After several days of heat there was a noticeable smell in the air and the deck boys began to complain. Eventually, in desperation and after a hasty service of farewell, a burial at sea was arranged. The story was not finished yet, though! Instead of sinking, the coffin remained afloat on the surface and with a change of wind direction, began to draw closer to the ship. The captain was horrified. What if passengers saw it! A ship haunted by a coffin! Someone suggested firing holes into the sides to make it sink. Another idea was to lower a tender, attach it to the coffin and tow it away at speed! Unfortunately, due perhaps to an excess of good red wine, our friend wasn't able to remember what happened in the end, but we all went to bed chuckling while trying to imagine a satisfactory conclusion.

Crew's wife on Tour

On one occasion, Nellie, the tour director, had asked me to escort a tour in the afternoon so, having checked with the Doc, who was on anchor watch, I spent my free morning ashore exploring the town. Originally anchor watch was the term used to describe crew-members whose job it was to stay on board and make sure the anchor didn't shift, but now it just meant the Doc had to spend time on board. Relieved not to have to watch anything he settled down in the afternoon to go through his notes, while I joined the tour group on the quay and counted my twenty-eight passengers on to the coach like a busy mother hen. Being a tour escort gives me the opportunity for a free tour but it's not always an easy option. I must make sure everyone on my coach is on the right tour and that they are all comfortable. I also check that they can hear the local guide's commentary at the back. If anyone is taken ill I have to find a taxi and take him or her back to the ship.

Two elderly ladies were a bit unsteady on their feet and I decided to keep an eye on them. The rain started as we arrived at Orchid World and Jeanne, our guide, went to the shop to borrow large umbrellas for everyone. Orchid World is towards the middle of the island of Barbados in the area known as St George. It used to be a chicken and pig farm but now it is a lovely orchid park.

Although not the main orchid season, there were a great variety of single specimen plants of delicate colours and other flowering shrubs too, so there was plenty to see. Going to investigate a slight commotion at the back of the group, I found a man had fallen backwards into an irrigation ditch while taking a photograph and I stopped to help him. He wasn't hurt, thank goodness, and only had wet feet. Back in the shop I found Jeanne gasping tears into her mobile phone.

"My mother has just died," she sobbed. Horrified to think she even started the tour at all I begged her to leave us and go home.

"We can manage and the driver knows where to go," I said, hopefully..

While the passengers had a look around the shop and visited the necessary facilities, I tried to comfort Jeanne while someone organised a taxi for her. We said a sad goodbye and then continued the tour with Barnabas, our driver, who combined his erratic driving skills with a spirited history of Barbados in a strong local dialect. I loved him for trying but couldn't understand a word he said!

Sunbury Plantation House, our next destination, was built in 1660 by an Irishman called Matthew Chapman who developed a great sugar estate around it. One of the first settlers on Barbados, he married and had three sons who all bought land in the area. After his death the house was sold to another family who changed its name, added more gardens and bought more land. Two brothers bought it in 1775 and renamed it Sunbury after their home in Kent in England. One brother, John Henry Barrow, planted the first teak tree in Barbados and also 300 mahogany trees, some of which still survive in the garden. John Barrow's son inherited the plantation and was Colonel in Charge of the slave rebellion in 1816 during which Sunbury was badly damaged. It was sold again after the abolition of slavery, but although the slaves were free they needed the work and stayed on the estate for two years as slave apprentices.

The house survived hurricanes in 1788 and had its roof replaced and then there was a fire in 1995 when much of the original furniture and structure was destroyed. Now a historically listed building, it was rebuilt in 1996 and refurnished in its original style.

Several other coaches arrived at the same time as us so I enjoyed a wander round the garden first, looking at a collection of old carts and machinery used to cultivate the land, and left the house for later when there would be more room inside.

I found it a fascinating place to visit, full of memories of a gracious and long gone past. The rooms were large and well proportioned, built to get the maximum benefit from any wind. Slatted shutters opened out and upward to let in light and there were open arches instead of doors between rooms. A long, sunny room where the ladies would sit to do their embroidery had doors at each end so that cooling breezes could pass through. Refurnished from a variety of homes on the island it accurately reflected the lives of former colonial settlers and their families enhanced by pictures and photographs.

Back on board ship I returned my escort badge and the first aid bag and hastily filled in the form given to me at the beginning of the tour, hoping I'd ticked all the right boxes. I had to note the state of the coach, the loudspeaker system, the itinerary, the facilities and the ability of the driver. Some tact was called for here so I chose my words carefully and asked the ship's cruise director to send a letter of condolence to the local office of tourism for our guide.

Meanwhile the Doc has had a busy afternoon too. He'd sent a sick passenger to hospital in Bridgetown and had a meeting in the officers' mess with the housekeeping team. Next he accepted an invitation to the Oceans cocktail party in the Lido Lounge. The Oceans are a special group of passengers who cruise often and receive concessions like flowers and champagne in their cabins on arrival and cocktail parties like this one. Things don't seem to have gone so smoothly after this. At evening clinic, he found there were problems on the domestic front. The nurse in charge, Liz, was fed up because the management kept sending her short contract agency nurses and she had to train them. The new one, who is only here for 11 days, flew out with us on the plane and is disappointed with her notably chilly reception. There was also a sweet-natured nurse from the Philippines who helped to look after the crew but was not allowed to be on call. Liz was threatening to give in her notice and leave us in Nassau so he may have no nurses at all unless they send someone else! After dinner, it seemed a good idea to take a turn around the deck and do some relaxing stargazing before going to bed.

Sometimes tours do not always turn out as planned and on this particular one I was relieved that I wasn't an escort. The Doc had worked on the first leg of this world cruise as far as Capetown and we were doing the next two weeks of the cruise as passengers and then flying home from Mombasa.

For once we were free to do as we pleased so we booked a safari tour from Richard's Bay to the Hluhluwe

Umfolozi Game Park. We drove by coach from the port to the park entrance at Memorial Gate where we were met by game rangers in open top wagons. The morning's drive allowed us to see a variety of animals including a great many giraffes and elephants. As lunchtime approached we stopped at the Reserve Centre and enjoyed a South African barbecue called a 'brai' before joining our transport again for the afternoon viewing. It began to rain and the rangers stopped to hand out thick woollen blankets to keep us dry. The rain brought more animals including a white rhino and several hippos to the river and we lingered to watch them so it was already late afternoon when we returned to the entrance of the park at Memorial Gate.

On board our coach we settled down for the long drive back. Suddenly the coach lurched sideways and went into the ditch at the side of the road. "Get out Madam, Sirs," shouted the driver and we quickly responded. Outside it was easy to see the problem. Although the rain had stopped, the mud road was soft and sticky and we had skidded at the bottom of a very slippery hill. Our African guide sent urgent messages on his mobile all to no effect. "They will come with another bus in twenty minutes," he said. After a while a very small tractor appeared and attempts were made to pull the bus out of the ditch. "Useless," snorted one of the passengers. Dressed in safari kit with a large brimmed bush hat, I privately nicknamed him 'the Colonel'. On board ship I had seen him in the bar surrounded by other men with loud voices boasting of former travelling exploits.

Leaving him to direct the hapless driver and the guide, I joined the others who were walking slowly up the hill. At least the bus would be lighter if we were not on it when it was pulled out! By now it was getting dark and the event was not quite so amusing. Insects were finding us tasty so those who had brought cans of 'jungle juice' mosquito protection rummaged in handbags and brought it out, reluctantly sharing it around with those who hadn't. At six o'clock we huddled nervously together hoping that no wild animals would leap out of the bush. "What if we are here all night?" I thought. Presently 'the Colonel' reappeared.

"We shall have to walk to the main road" he announced in a military voice. "Men in front and at the rear, and women in the centre. Has anyone got a torch?"

Although his intentions were good there were several objections. "We don't know how far it is," someone said. A few of the passengers had walking sticks and the more elderly were plainly unable to walk anywhere. Unable to keep silent any longer the Doc vetoed the suggestion firmly. Although not there in an official capacity he would obviously be the one called upon should anyone collapse.

Enveloped in warm darkness I stood apart from the others. I could smell a sweet earthy smell and hear the rustle of some small animal nearby. It was a novel experience to be standing on a road in the middle of the African countryside at night and one I knew would probably never happen to me again.

Our rescue came quickly after that. There was a lot of crunching of gears and grinding noises and a column of battered vehicles came slowly up the hill towards us, headlights wobbling on the bumpy road. Local farmers from all around had brought their lorries and trucks and come to find us. Ignoring the Colonel, who was trying to make some kind of ordered queue, they picked up the elderly passengers and dumped them in the back of the trucks then the rest of us piled in after them, crouching wherever there was space. The men travelled standing in the cattle wagons, their silhouettes swaying to and fro in the darkness as the convoy made a careful return to the tarmac surface of the main road. There, a replacement coach was waiting for us.

It was ten-thirty when we arrived at the ship's gangway, relieved to find ourselves back on board and that there was some food prepared for us. Within minutes we heard the engines spring to life and we left Richard's Bay for our next port of call, six hours later than planned.

St Helena

"Will it be calm enough to land?" I ask the First Engineer anxiously. Over a period of five years, our cruise ship had only been able to send tenders ashore twice at St Helena. This tropical island has a total landmass of 47 square miles and is about 1,000 miles off the West African coast. Its nearest neighbours are two small islands, Ascension and Tristan da Cunha, themselves also dependencies of Great Britain.

I felt a strange empathy with this island. My father had visited it en-route to South Africa in 1924 and had left me a diary in which he described his twenty-five day journey. On board a Union Castle liner, the Royal Navy had sent him to join a new ship berthed in the Naval Dockyard in Simonstown near Capetown. The ship called at St Helena and Ascension Islands and he described how horrified the passengers were to see bullocks kept penned in the forepart of the ship being released here. After being tied with a rope around their horns, each animal was slung out on derricks and dropped into the water where boats were waiting to tow them into shore.

Even today there was only a tiny landing stage and no sheltering seawall around the harbour. In a choppy sea or with a rough swell boats would get smashed to pieces. At tender level, once we had leapt aboard the pitching boat, we nervously looked up at the formidable cliffs plunging vertiginously into the deep water. It was hard to see how anyone could survive on the treeless mountains that form a jagged silhouette against the skyline. No wonder it was considered a suitable place of exile for Napoleon Bonaparte in 1815 after his defeat at the Battle of Waterloo.

I had to make the short journey without the Doc who had a seriously ill passenger on board. He had managed to get one of the two local resident, medical officers from the General Hospital on St Helena to return on the tender so they could share expertise. Sadly there is no airport on the island and sending the patient ashore here to be repatriated was not possible. RMS St Helena, the supply ship, was not due until well after we arrived in Namibia, our next port of call, so we had to keep the sick man on board.

There was no beach to be seen along the coastline and only a tin shed when we leapt ashore at the wharf. The welcome was unconditional, however, as a sun-tanned man stepped forward from the waiting group, his face creasing into a huge smile. English is widely spoken on St Helena although normally at a much faster speed. Consequently it was quite difficult to understand what he was saying but easy to realise that he was pleased to see us. The locals indulged us and spoke slowly as if we were all slightly deaf. We followed them along a wide gravel path leading to town, walking in the footsteps of Napoleon, The Duke of Wellington, Captain Bligh, Arthur Haley, Charles Darwin, Captain James Cook, and yes, probably, my father too. I felt like a royal personage with all these people nodding and smiling at me. In front of us was Jacob's Ladder, built in 1829, with seven hundred steps to its six hundred foot summit.

I decided to enter the town by its more traditional route, through an archway guarding a sunlit square beyond. Above the archway entrance was the East India Coat of Arms and on the other side, the Wirebird, the island's national bird. This bird is like a small plover and builds its nest on the ground. To deter predators from finding its eggs it runs away rapidly dragging one wing as if it's broken. Wirebirds are native to St Helena and are becoming rare so I hoped we might see one during our stay.

The East India Company built the first settlement here in 1657 when the island became an important fortress and staging post on the way home from India. Named Jamestown after King James II, the island's capital is well prepared for visiting cruise ships, though its inhabitants must also be used to arrangements having to be cancelled due to the weather. Today in St James' church they were providing free refreshments and the shop doors along Main Street were open for us to peer inside. The locals were as interested in us as we were in them and stood or sat in the sunshine eager to talk and answer our questions. Their faces showed traces of their many ancestors including British settlers, Chinese and Indians brought out by the East India Company to work in the coaling station, and Boers and Zulus from the wars in South Africa. There were also Madagascans, Malays and freed West African slaves and finally Marines from Great Britain who were sent to guard Napoleon after he was defeated at Waterloo.

Looking around the main square reminded me of Toy Town in the television series so loved by my own children when they were small. The council offices were housed in a miniature castle near the library, the police station, and adjacent courthouse, all neatly labelled above their entrances. We peered nosily through the bars of the gaol

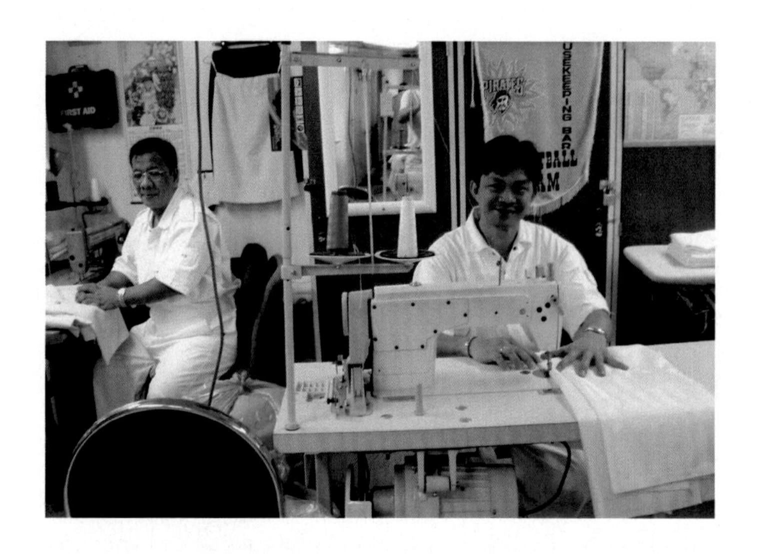

Tailors at work Deck 2 Black Watch

Survivor at Sea, crew training

Crossing the Line Ceremony, dumping the Captain

Paramedic being lowered for Medical Evacuation

Seaman working below deck

Walking Tour group enjoying lunch in the mountains Norway

Medical Team and equipment

Peter the Great's Cottage St Petersburg

Having a little swim before sailing. Grand Turk

Iceberg off the coast of Greenland

Preparing dinner in the Galley

Local people selling their goods Nosy Be Madagascar

Selling Herbs and Spices Hellville Market

Shy Fox in Tierra del Fuego N.P. Patagonia-Argentine

Bryggen, Bergen, Norway

Gala Buffet

The Ice Dolphin Grand Buffet

but there seemed to be only two prisoners inside who smiled and waved at us. Afterwards we found out that they were hardly real criminals and had been locked up following drunk and disorderly conduct the night before. In Main Street there were several Regency houses now offering Bed and Breakfast, and a few small shops selling groceries and other essentials. One shop had a good selection of island grown coffee and I bought some to take home. I also got postcards in the Post Office and wrote them on the balcony of the Consulate Hotel opposite. (There was no hurry to post them. As there is no airport, they will not leave the island until three weeks later on RMS St Helena and we will be home long before they reach their destinations.) Then we strolled up Napoleon Street, so named because the Emperor had to go this way to reach The Briars, where he spent the first five months of his imprisonment.

In the afternoon the Doc joined me, and we shared a taxi with another couple to explore the interior of the island. Our vehicle, a large open-backed truck, was not the most comfortable over the bumpy roads but had the advantage of giving us good views all around. Jamestown itself is situated in a deep, volcanic valley with rocky slopes on each side so, as we left it, the interior of the island turned out to be a delightful surprise. The roads were single lanes with passing places and on each side there were neat hillside meadows with grazing cows and little pens of sheep outside tiny wooden farmhouses with flower-decked verandas. Cacti, New Zealand flax, Palm trees and tropical flowers mingled with wild agapanthus and nasturtiums in the valley where Napoleon's tomb still stands, though his remains have long since been claimed by the French and removed to Paris. Longwood House, his last home while he was detained on the island, is now a museum and much of the original furniture is on display. His canopied bed was pathetically small. Even for a short man, its diminutive size must have forced him to sleep curled up in it. To stave off boredom, Napoleon designed a garden around the house using his guards to help with the heavy work. They would certainly otherwise be under-employed. The garden had sunken paths, a pond and a gazebo. Like most tourists who visit St Helena I was fascinated by his story. The manner of his death on 5th May 1821 is still disputed and some think he was poisoned.

We entered the Governor's Residence, Plantation House, through a kissing gate. Despite its interesting name, a kissing gate is really only a small gate that swings between a vee-shaped enclosure and touches each side so that only one person can pass at a time. Made that way to prevent animals getting through, it has acquired a reputation of being a place where a lady, having been handed through the gate by her partner, then demanded a kiss before allowing him to follow her. The house itself was built in 1792 as a country residence for the Governor of the Honourable East India Company but is now mainly famous for its animal inhabitants, especially Jonathan the tortoise, who is reputed to be over 150 years old. His four companions, Emma, David, Myrtle and Frederica ambled around us looking equally ancient so it was difficult to decide which was, in fact, Jonathan. We took photos of the unusual garden residents and of the house from the lawn, and climbed up into our taxi wagon, grateful that the driver made a comfort stop at a small public toilet block about thirty metres along the road. We had debated knocking on the door of Plantation House!

As we made our way homewards to Jamestown, we passed places with names evocative of the past and I longed to stay and find out more about them: High Knoll Fort, Lot and Lot's Wife, with Half Tree Hollow all had a tale to tell, but we didn't have time to linger. We ended our tour at the top of Jacob's ladder, built as an inclined plane to haul up manure from Jamestown and take goods down. Holding firmly to the handrail, we descended in late afternoon sunlight arriving just in time for tea in a small café before making our way back to the wharf steps.

When we sailed that evening, we were cheered and waved on our way by the islanders, many of whom were probably descendants of those who waved to my father on that Union Castle liner in the spring of 1924.

Keeping Fit not Fat

There was absolutely no reason why I should not keep fit on board. The ship had a well-equipped gym that I kept meaning to explore. One morning I got motivated and walked up the eight flights of stairs to the top deck. There was an energetic movement class in progress and I watched from the sidelines as fifteen or sixteen people stretched and bent to music trying not to fall over when the ship wobbled a bit. There was a Pilates class next and I joined in, lying full length on a mat with my nose pressed into the floor while I tried to follow Orlando's instructions.

Orlando, from Eastern Europe, is tall and handsome with a physique I might have envied were I a male. Trying to hold my stomach muscles, my central core (what is that?) at 30 percent, while simultaneously lifting and lowering my left leg was giving me cramp and I rolled over and bumped into the lady next to me. We giggled and started again. Most participants were female but there were a few men on the edge of the group. We kept going for forty minutes and finally got to do the bit I like, relaxation: We lay flat on our backs and closed our eyes while breathing deeply. All I could think about was the long cool glass of fruit punch I was going to have on deck in about fifteen minutes.

If I got up at eight in the morning I could join the

'Walk a Mile with a Smile' group. Just walking round this ship's wide scrubbed decks five times is a popular way to walk a mile a day. Most people do it later after breakfast and in fine weather it was so popular that signs were erected to tell us all to walk in the same clockwise direction to save accidentally bumping into passengers going the other way.

The gym also had a collection of items to trim and exercise every muscle. I decided to try the rowing machine and spent fifteen minutes trying to fathom out how it worked. This was my own fault for not paying attention to the introductory session I had recently undergone. However the rowing machine was fun once you got the hang of it, especially if you were on your own in the gym which is when I like to be there. I sing "Speed Bonny Boat" as I swing along dreamily watching the evening sky outside slowly change from pink to purple as the ship dips and rises on the waves. It's a different matter when the sea's rough of course, but I tended to avoid the gym then and find a corner in the library to while away the hours with a book in a comfortable armchair. The other machine I tried was much more taxing and certainly required more concentration if it was not to run away with me. It was a moving platform that could be set to different speeds. You could even alter the tilt and walk uphill on it. The entertainment staff used it regularly and perfected the art of running at speed and not holding on at all. I started at a very sedate walking speed but even so nearly fell off when I forgot to keep moving as someone marching along on the machine next to me started chatting. Afterwards I went through the motions, wiping away non-existent sweat and filling my paper cup from the water fountain, but really I know I'm a fraud! I left the weights; exercise bikes and other paraphernalia to more dedicated enthusiasts and decided to stick to strolling on deck and trying not to eat too much delicious food. The problem was that the special afternoon teas on days at sea are very difficult to avoid. They were served in several places simultaneously and as fast as you hurried past one table laden with cream cakes and mouthwatering doughnuts, you walked slap bang into another where your friends were smiling and waving for you to join them.

As I like walking at home and the Doc likes golf we try to find similar exercise ashore when we get the chance, and if it's not possible we try something new.

One day on Bornholm, an island off the coast of Denmark, we were persuaded to hire real bicycles and go for an afternoon forest ride with one of the nurses. Kath was very fit and slim and soon left us behind. Fortunately, the terrain was flat and made for easy cycling, but you did need to keep your eyes open for stray logs in the middle of the path, excitable dogs not quite under their owners control, while also listening for faster cyclists hovering behind you. I hadn't ridden a bicycle for many years and felt rather nervous, stopping frequently to let others pass. This wasn't a good idea because I kept falling off when the brakes jammed as I stopped peddling. At the edge of the forest we arrived at a small quay where Kath was waiting for us. She wouldn't be cajoled into a rest and refreshment stop but shot off on the return journey, anxious to get back to the ship. We took longer but my confidence improved and I didn't wobble as much on the way back. I was sorry to hand the bikes in at the end of our trip but realised that, although I'd enjoyed the ride, I had been concentrating so hard on keeping upright I had no idea about the island scenery we had just ridden through. It could have been anywhere in the world.

A cruise ship may not be an ideal place for cycling but there is never any need to be bored on the long days at sea. The enthusiastic entertainments team are constantly devising games and encouraging passengers to try a variety of unusual activities no one has ever heard of before. As well as these there's table tennis, short tennis and golf nets on the upper deck and of course the warm swimming pools, a deep tank where your swimming strokes push against a moving current and Jacuzzis for those who prefer the more relaxing option. If you are not a physically active person you can play cards, chess, scrabble, darts or join the arts and crafts classes and learn how to paint, sew and make small souvenirs to take home.

I'm not very good at any of these but agreed to join a group playing quoits on deck one long summer evening in the Northern hemisphere. Quoits are small rings made of some raffia-like material that you have to throw along the deck into marked squares to gain points. Being left handed my quoits inevitably landed in the sea and I eventually ended up being the least popular member of my team. I was embarrassed at having to go to the reception desk to collect more supplies but on my return I found the game had ended. An irate lady trying to sleep in her cabin had complained that our noisy game outside the window was keeping her awake. It was only then that we realised that despite being still bright daylight it was nearly midnight.

The dance classes that usually take place in the afternoons were always very popular but I avoided these. There are partners available to dance with single women but I feel it's unfair to take advantage of them when I do have my own partner, just not one who is available. I did try line dancing but found that my tendency to turn right when I should have turned left ruined the whole sequence for everybody else. I love ballroom dancing though, so sometimes, late at night, I enticed the Doc up on the top deck and we danced together all alone in the moonlight. We could hear the music from the deck below and I tried to convince him it was good exercise and that officers need to be fit! He tolerates a slow waltz but after one or two lively quicksteps around the stacks of sun loungers he's likely to complain plaintively, "I walk up and down eight flights of stairs all the day long, can we go to bed now?"

South Africa: Coming into Capetown

The mournful sound of fog hooters accompanied us as the ship crept slowly towards Capetown. I was on the bridge with the Doc, a special treat. I felt I should really be wearing an elegant dress and dainty hat instead of my shorts and tee shirt, as I hovered behind the officers in their gold-embellished white uniforms. I stood in the warm, damp mist, camera poised, waiting hopefully for the sun to break through. It seemed unlikely, but suddenly, in front of my eyes, the white curtain of fog lifted, and there was the city, shining white in bright sunlight, with Table Mountain behind, outlined against a brilliant blue sky. I felt so exhilarated that I could hardly breathe and, as we drew closer, my camcorder went into overdrive. Small boats whizzed past, sails flapping in the brisk breeze and our pilot boat puttered gently alongside hooting a warning at them. Overhead, hundreds of sea birds wheeled and dived, and a seaplane flew right above the ship trailing a welcome banner. As we entered the harbour, I saw several seals that had appropriated the large black tyres placed against the harbour walls to protect ships. They lolled there in the sun in whiskery contentment, not even opening one eye to look up at us.

We only had a few days to explore this part of South Africa and we filled it with enough experiences to last a lifetime. We berthed in the Victoria and Alfred

Waterfront, an amazing amalgamation of harbour, tourist shopping malls, restaurants and open-air entertainment. As soon as the ship was cleared I hurried down the gangway straight on to the quay. I paused to listen to some local musicians and laughed at the clowns doing juggling tricks in the little stone bays, with benches provided for their audience. At the far end, historic buildings mixed with an aquarium, an Imax cinema and dozens of small restaurants overlooking motorboats whose owners touted loudly for trade. By now it was mid morning and getting hot, so I rested for a moment in the shade of a Dragon Tree whose sap, known as dragon's blood, was said to have been used by sailors to treat dysentery and diarrhoea.

The Doc had a patient in hospital here. The medical team had nursed him carefully during five long days at sea following our visit to St Helena. I had taken turns to sit with him and keep his wife company in the afternoons until we reached Walvis Bay in Namibia, where a plane was waiting to fly him to Capetown for specialist treatment. Now that our ship had arrived the Doc had arranged to visit him. Not only would it be good to see him but it was also an opportunity to have a peep at one of South Africa's well-known private clinics.

Rather than exploring alone, I decided to join friends who were going to the top of Table Mountain in the cable car. A taxi took us to the base of the mountain. Each cable car took sixty people and revolved slowly so that everyone got to see the view. We were lucky it was a clear day and we didn't notice how windy it was until we stepped out at the top. My companion, Mariella, wailed as her dress blew over her head and gave everyone a good view of her tanned thighs and well-known department store underwear. Strolling along a path on the edge of the cliff, we could look down at our tiny cruise ship in the harbour and see the coastline along the whole sweep of the bay. There were dainty humming birds in the heathery plants on the edge of the path and a lizard skittered across in front of us. I couldn't find any of the indigenous mice that were supposed to look like miniature elephants. "They probably only come out at night,." Mariella surmised.

On the way down in the cable car I wriggled my way to the front and had an amazing 360-degree view of the city as we went round and round. Back in the centre, I left the others to explore a department store, lured in by the cheap prices advertised in the window. Stepping inside to wander along the rails of dresses in front of me I suddenly realised I was the only white person among the throngs of African women in the store. This was a new experience for me and gave me a small inkling of what it must be like to be a new immigrant in my own country.

Rejoining the others we walked together the whole length of the Company's Garden. Owned by the East India Company, it was first planted in the 1650s by European settlers, to provide fresh produce for passing ships, but is now an ornamental and popular tourist attraction. A long straight row of grand buildings stretched the length of the gardens, among them the South African Museum, the Art gallery and Parliament Building. Statues of famous people, incongruous with local pigeons perched on their heads, were dotted here and there and beneath them groups of unemployed men lay sleeping the day away on the grass. Already the end of summer, many of the flowers were over but there were still some brightly lit areas where the African flame trees glowed red against the sky and other corners where gaudy blooms showed off amongst the seed heads.

Exhausted with the heat, we finally reached Mount Nelson Hotel, resplendent in strawberry pink paint. Hoping we would pass muster in our crumpled touring clothes, we ordered afternoon tea on the balcony. It was a little cooler there and tea was a delight: sandwiches, biscuits and cakes in true English fashion and a large pot of tea. It was both equally fascinating and then irritating to listen to the loud voices of the couple on the table behind us, who were doing business deals over their mobile phones. While they discussed their millions we felt poor and humble but grateful that we too could afford afternoon tea at 125 rands each, unlike the sleeping men we had just passed in the park.

The next day, with the Doc free at last, we explored the city from the top of an open deck tour bus, trying to remember to duck our heads to avoid being hit by low branches in the tree-lined streets. The Waterfront was built on reclaimed land, together with most of the prosperous city behind it and we had a good view of both from the top of Signal hill. On the outskirts of Capetown we passed blocks of new houses and flats for local people, some of whom had reluctantly been moved there from their original shantytown homes.

On another bus we drove the scenic route alongside the Atlantic Ocean between Camps Bay and Hout Bay, home to a fleet of fishing vessels, and known for its crayfish, Cape Rock Lobster. Then passing through the green and lush wine-producing valley of Constancia, we took the Ou Kaapse Weg (the old Cape Road) to Simonstown.

We stopped at Boulders Beach where family groups

were sharing their packed lunches with a colony of penguins. Each bird sat on her egg in a hole in the sand, opening and closing her beak slowly to help keep cool. Others waddled importantly up and down in and out of the picnics, or meandered down to the sea for a swim. They amused us by stealing anything they could find and wandering off with it to the nest. Sunglasses, food, clothing and anything else small enough was filched from the careless piles left on the sand. Children were enjoying the game of chasing them and bringing back the stolen goods.

In Simonstown, where my father had once been based during his naval career, I craned my neck to see over the high granite wall of the Naval Dockyard. The buildings inside looked so similar to the Naval Bases at Portsmouth and Plymouth that the whole complex could have been picked up and dropped there on a magic carpet straight from England.

From the lighthouse on the Cape of Good Hope we gazed down into the Indian Ocean. Somewhere here, the warm Mozambique and cold Benguela currents meet and cause changes to the forms of marine life in the water and the flora on the peninsula. I imagined the warm air above them mingling and in a momentary silence, as the group of people near me moved away, I almost felt the ghost of my sailor Dad standing close behind me, and the soft whisper of his breath blowing gently on my neck. If I turned my head, I could imagine his blue eyes looking intently at the water below trying like me to detect the invisible join in the sea. On our drive back through the National Park the Doc shouted, "Look over there." Groups of monkeys were leaping over tussocks of grass as if they were trying to race the bus and a group of pernickety ostriches at the edge of the road, swivelled their tiny heads in concert, as we passed.

On our last morning in Capetown we booked a cruise to Robben Island. It was to change my whole perception of the idyllic tourist country we had seen so far. The boat was late leaving but eventually we all shuffled forward through the security system and climbed on board for the six-kilometre journey.

Since the end of the 17th century, Robben Island has been used to isolate people, mainly prisoners, and amongst its first permanent inhabitants were political leaders from various Dutch colonies. The island was also used as a leper colony and as a place to quarantine animals, but the reason most visitors like us are drawn to it is to see the place where Nelson Mandela spent much of his twenty-seven years in prison for opposing apartheid. Stopping to take a photograph of the entrance I had to hurry to catch up with the others as they were led into the prison yard, a bare concrete area surrounded by high walls and then into one of the long rows of wooden huts lining the yard. Each cell contained a plank bed, a bucket and a stool. In the hot, stuffy building we were met by a former inmate who told us what it had been like to live there as a political prisoner. Now he was a guide and spoke in measured tones to make sure we did not miss any of his words. In one cell, he showed us letters from other prisoners, idealistic South Africans who dreamt of a world where they were free to do the things they wanted alongside their white compatriots. We learned that along with other prominent ANC members, Mandela and his friend Walter Sisulu supported fellow prisoners until they could be released. They named the prison a kind of Open University and set up classes for anyone who wanted to learn at any level. It was sobering to hear that the lowest categories of prisoners, political activists, were allowed only one visitor and one letter every six months. Even these letters were often delayed and spoilt by the censors.

Outside, we were led to the lime quarry where prisoners had to do hard labour. It must have been sheer torture breaking up stone by hand in searing midday heat. Many prisoners also suffered eye damage from the glaring sunlight. We walked in silence around the leper graveyard, a sad and melancholy place. On our way to the exit, I dropped behind to ask the guide why, now that he was free, he stayed there working in a place with such terrible memories.

He shrugged and replied, "There is no other work for me."

On our return journey the Doc and I felt subdued. We were relieved to board our comfortable, floating home once more and I realised with a tired sigh that I was glad we would soon be moving on. The enigma of South Africa was just too difficult to understand in three days.

Food and Fun

Cocktail parties are an endless form of entertainment on board. On our cruise ships the Captain gives one at the beginning and end of each cruise and there are others, exclusive to the members of various clubs and agencies, on board. If, like some passengers, you are on board for fifty-three days, it would be possible to attend at least sixteen cocktail parties with goodness knows how many Pina Colodas, Rum Punches, sherries or Martinis, to match: and all this, before a five-course dinner. Most passengers enjoy the opportunity to dress up, though I suspect that the men are not quite so comfortable in rarely-used dinner suits fitting a little too snugly. While the band plays softly and the Captain and Officers stand in line to greet everyone, I lurk in the background like an abandoned wallflower trying not to help myself to too many hors-d'oeuvres.

One evening as the Doc left the stage after the Captain's formal introductions, a retired Naval gentleman in the audience roundly rebuked him. "Do you know that your bottom button is undone, sir?" The Doc looked down wondering if his trousers were in order. "Your jacket," the man hissed. It was no good protesting that his stethoscope wouldn't fit in the silly little pocket, the medical Officer was improperly dressed! After that, prior to similar functions I stood at the cabin door brandishing a clothes brush and we had an inspection before going on show.

For the waiters, dinner is always difficult on the first night of a cruise. The passengers are new and often go to sit at the wrong table or don't like where they are placed and want to change. Others want a table for two and then find that they don't like it after all and want to join others they may have just met. By the end of the first sitting, the staff has got into the swing. The head waiter has reassured two couples about their choice of wine, replaced three meals which had been apparently ordered wrongly and comforted one of his assistants who was certain he had not made a mistake. He has arranged for a change of table for one couple and a change of sitting for another three people who want to eat at the later time. He's checked to see that the wine is uncorked and ready for the next sitting and at the end of the meal he stands by the exit smiling as the diners, replete and in a jolly mood, make their way out.

On one of the 'round the world' cruises on which the Doc was working for a month, we had the chance to get to know some of the waiters. Mephisto was our wine waiter. Dark-haired and suave, he waited to be fallen in love with by all the solo ladies. He presented the house red as if it were a precious antique and the men nodded solemnly as they completed the tasting ritual. Our table waiter was called Victor. His role as the star singer in the crew show the night before had gone to his head and he revelled in everyone's well-deserved congratulations. Because of this he wasn't concentrating very well and got the orders confused. Tonight, in mid-conversation, we thanked him briefly for our main course and then looking down realised that it looked different because he had mistakenly given us pheasant. Somewhere else in the dining room equally absorbed diners were tucking into our lamb chops. Because he had such appealing brown eyes and the Head Waiter was glaring, we gave in and ate pheasant, but declined the mint sauce. He rewarded us by giving us extra attention and re-filled our water glasses every two minutes. As soon as we were finished, our plates were whisked away and the table de-crumbed. Victor made sure the desserts reached the correct destinations as we embarked on the fourth, or was it fifth, course? At this stage, replete with food and wine I was on automatic pilot and didn't really care what I was eating, especially as the conversation was going well.

All the waiters seemed to work extremely hard. Knowing I was keeping a diary, the Senior Waiter filled in a sheet labelled 'Twenty-four hours in the life of ? ' for me. It began:

1.00am to 5.00am	Watching TV/Video and sleeping.
5.00am	Time to get up and prepare all the things needed for the day
6.00am	Reporting for duty and preparing the restaurant (if everything in order)
7.00am	Check all tables and all waiters in post
8.00am	Time for breakfast
9.00am	Go for break if one of the waiters will come to relieve me
10.00am	Sleeping

11.00am	Back to restaurant to set up buffet table for lunch
12.00noon	Open restaurant, do service and take wine orders for lunch and dinner
1.00pm	Guiding diners to tables and serving.
2.00pm	Open wines ordered from lunch in time for 1st sitting dinner
3.00pm	Afternoon break/sleeping
4.30pm	Get up, shower, prepare dinner service in restaurant
5.00pm	Put wines ordered on respective tables
6.00pm	Attend daily restaurant meeting
6.30pm	Restaurant open for 1st sitting
7.00pm	Serving diners
8.00pm	Serving and preparing wines for 2nd sitting at 8.30pm
9.00pm	Serving diners
10.00pm	Night break and changing uniform for midnight buffet
11.00pm	Check restaurant and open midnight buffet at 11.30pm
12.00 midnight	Close the restaurant. Check everything is cleared and clean.

Each new cruise brings us new dinner guests. Edward from Tewksbury was a retired bachelor. A large man with a mellifluous voice, he was resigned to misfortune aboard ship and indeed he was always the man who lost his cabin key, slipped on deck or whose deckchair collapsed under him. His sentences finished with a loud, sonorous "Ah well". He seemed to be unaware of his habit of snorting loudly too, which got a bit wearisome by the time we reached the dessert course. Lily, a solo traveller too, was seventy-nine and looked younger than me. She lived in a modern flat in Bournemouth and told us she is claustrophobic. "I put wedges under my doors and windows at home to keep them open so that I don't feel shut in," she told me. Unable to contemplate flying she had cruised all over the world but, when I asked which was her favourite place, she couldn't remember. "After a while they all look the same," she trilled happily. This was her fiftieth cruise and her last, but her smile disappeared as she stated, "Standards have dropped".

I didn't pursue this discussion because I knew I would get a long line of complaints and I didn't want to spoil my own personal contentment. I was still at the euphoric stage where I thought everything here was wonderful.

Our favourite co-diners are those who are good fun, always buy their share of the wine and never talk about their ailments. Albert and Joan were from the north of England and this was their third cruise. They really entered into the spirit of everything on board and were determined to enjoy themselves. They went to a ballroom dancing class in the afternoon and regaled us at dinner with their efforts to learn the Salsa and the Merengue. The dance tutor was tall and lean and his ability to wiggle his hips was copied by Albert as he headed the queue to enter the dining room. He soon had me laughing as I tried to join in. Later in the cruise Joan won the passenger talent contest and came first in the Ascot fancy dress hats competition. On the last evening, they unfortunately chose to describe their one and only night of seasickness while we were all tackling the mulligatawny soup. I quickly tried to change the subject and Albert told us a joke instead.

A Small Taste of Paradise

On Caribbean cruises there are so many islands to choose from that there is always somewhere different to go. Today we were visiting one of the Turks and Caicos, a group of eight islands and forty small cays. They lie about 575 miles southeast of Miami and are divided into groups separated by the Columbus Passage. To the west is the Caicos group and to the east, where we were going, is the Turks group; Grand Turk and Salt Cay. We were being tendered ashore and from the ship the long flat island of Grand Turk looked deserted, but there were concrete bunker-like buildings behind the beach and from the centre of the island a tall slender radio mast denoted the presence of the Cable and Wireless Company. There's a small wooden jetty with a fishing boat anchored nearby, but no harbour.

Below me the red and white tendering boats bobbed up and down in the water. There was a slight swell and the passengers lining the ship's rail, craned their necks to peer doubtfully at the stairway and platform projecting from the side of the ship. We waited for clearance, impatient to be off in case the swell should increase. After a day at sea it would be good to get our feet on solid ground again. The diesel-fumed air in the tender set a few people spluttering but we soon arrived at the jetty. To our surprise there was a one-man band waiting to greet us.

He was standing, cluttered with instruments, between a huge pair of amplifiers. His jolly calypso music followed me along the beach as I set off to explore.

Because I walked faster than the others I arrived at the town first. Cockburn is the Capital of the Turks and Caicos Islands but seemed to be deserted. For once I was alone and the first street was silent and empty. The concrete road surface was covered with a fine layer of sand so my feet made no sound. On either side there were handmade, stone walls, broken in places and patched up with wooden palings. Wooden shacks hid in small gardens, their shuttered windows peeping out through the tangled vegetation. There were no palm trees but the branches of sturdy pine-trees cast shade. The heat was dazzling and I was tempted to creep under a purple-flowered pergola, through which the flowers of deep-blue Morning Glory flowers forced themselves skywards. On the other side the white beach came right up to the road. It was strewn with pink and white conch shells and small pieces of coloured glass worn smooth by the waves. The sea was an unbelievable aquamarine, so clear that if I gazed long enough I would be able to see the sting rays shovelling their huge, flat bodies along the sandy shoreline.

Around the corner I found the Post Office. It was a decrepit, colonial building with a long wooden veranda on the second floor. Its paint was faded and peeling in keeping with its sleepy surroundings. Inside, a paddle fan turned slowly in the ceiling stirring the warm air, but the man behind the counter was in no hurry. His face broke into a smile as he greeted me.

"Sorry I have no postcards, Ma'am," he told me, "but you can get one in the museum." I asked where the shops were and he shook with laughter. There are three on this island and I had passed two of them without knowing. Just as the town doesn't look like a town from my vantage point, the shops don't look like shops either. Eventually I found one down a small sandy alley but some passengers from the ship had already arrived before me. They were busy examining the pretty merchandise made of shells and driftwood. The longhaired, American owner told us he had had a concrete floor laid beneath the wooden one because of our combined weight. He only had room for nine customers at once and usually got about two a day. Ours was the first cruise ship to call for two years and I wondered how on earth he made a living here.

The museum was near the Grand Turk Treasury, which appeared to be sinking in the sand. It was a most insignificant shed to have such an important title and was firmly locked and shuttered, perhaps with all the treasure inside or more probably because it was no longer in use. My suspicions were confirmed when I turned the corner and came upon an enormous and very new branch of Barclays Bank. By then, hot and thirsty, I found a small hotel with green shutters and sipped Pina Colada under the trees in the company of a friendly black dog. At that moment I'd like to have stayed here among the butterflies for ever. The Museum, where I did buy my postcard, also contained artefacts from a wrecked ship that had sunk on the nearby Molasses Reef in 1513 and was believed to be the earliest ship found in the Americas.

The highest point of the island was a gentle climb through dry brushwood and cactus bushes. Small iguanas scuttled away indignantly as I approached the summit. From here you could see the sheer, deep-water drop-off between this and another island. It was clearly marked by a line of dark blue, while the shallower water outlined the islands with a lighter hue. I wondered about the people who had been there before me. The island natives are descendants of African slaves brought here to work in the salt-mines. American Loyalist planters also came here and cargo ships supplied them with food. Nowadays, the islands are renowned for diving and deep-sea fishing. Turning to retrace my steps, I watched straggling groups of passengers making their way in noontime heat along the un-shaded track. They looked like refugees, clutching beach towels and plastic bottles of water. Back at the jetty, the one-man band still playing, there was just time to plunge into the sea for a swim before boarding the tender. Paddling into the water I scuffed the sand with my feet to send any lurking stingrays on their way.

Not So Safe Places

In the enclosed and comfortable environment of 'on board' it's easy to become complacent. Despite regular warnings in the daily newsletters about taking care when going ashore, we are often so absorbed by the initial drama and excitement of a new country that we forget that not everything may be quite what it seems.

After several days at sea during our Atlantic crossing it was a relief to see the Cape Verde Islands coming into view. The scenery of black volcanic cliffs dropping straight into the sea didn't give a very welcoming impression but I took a photo anyway. We were about to land at Mindelo, the capital of the island of Sao Vincente. We berthed in the deep-water port of Porto Grande, which is connected to Mindelo Bay by an underwater volcanic crater. It was ideal for cruise ships and other commercial traffic. Formerly colonised by Portugal, Mindelo became a prosperous supply station in the 19th century. Provisions of imported coal, water and livestock were sold to ships and ocean liners using the Atlantic shipping lanes. In 1885 Mindelo was the switching station for the first transatlantic telegraph cable. Nowadays fishing and tourism are the main means of making a living.

Beyond the port, there were large, beautiful houses with satellite dishes etched against the skyline. The landscape looked very arid and I was surprised to see camels grazing on the steep slopes – somehow, they didn't go with the satellite dishes. When the ship docked we watched from the rails as a crowd of determined young men swiftly dismantled a large skip full of the ship's discarded rubbish and carried it away. Old tables, broken chairs, coat hangers, and empty oil drums were their first choice, but nothing was wasted.

As we were only docked here for a short time, I travelled into town with other passengers on the free shuttle bus and then wandered around on my own. The streets in the town centre were littered with rubbish but the colonial buildings were in good repair. Some still had the original Portuguese flag and dates of building above the door. With the help of my ship's street guide I found the Centro National de Artisanato but it was closed. I had hoped to see some local art, ceramics and wooden artefacts that the port lecturer had told us about on board. I viewed the tower of Belem from the outside. It's a copy of the one in Lisbon and not really very exciting. My favourite place was the municipal market. Mesmerised by the display of fruit and vegetables I was startled when a German tourist stopped me and advised me in hesitant English to turn my rucksack around. "Let it sit on front and not the back," he said earnestly. Before this I had felt quite safe on my own. The people around me seemed to be busy buying and selling their wares but there were probably some who were watching me as intently as I was observing them. Mostly female, they were basically of African origin, probable descendants of the slaves who were brought to the islands in the 16th century to work on Portuguese plantations. Refugees from Europe escaping religious persecution joined them. Their features varied in colour from very dark to light coffee colour and one or two had blonde hair and blue eyes. The fruit and vegetables mainly came from other islands, especially Santo Antao, which had a more humid climate. Later, after meeting up with the Doc for a drink in a small kiosk, we decided to walk back to the docks instead of waiting for a bus. As we left the town and strolled along the seafront road to the port, there was a sudden commotion ahead. A metal barrier was dragged across the road in front of us. Terrified that we were going to be mugged, we tried to hide behind an upturned boat but the assailants were not interested in us. They had been lying in wait for another skip full of rubbish being driven away from the ship. As the lorry skidded to a halt, they attacked the men on the back with sticks and metal poles, at the same time knocking down goods that appealed to them. The battle was over in a few minutes. Grabbing whatever they could carry, the robbers ran away and the lorry inched slowly forward over the barrier with a grinding crunch. Shaken, we scuttled out from our hiding place and walked back to our ship very quickly. I tried to avoid the eye of a young lad wearing a blue bin bag as a shirt who tried to sell me some wooden beads he was wearing on his arm. Another time I may well have stopped to talk with him. At the bottom of the gangway we met a man in a wheelchair with no shoes on his feet. Passengers were passing down a variety of footwear for him to try on. I hoped that by the time we sailed he would have enough shoes for a second hand stall in the market in town.

I usually try to wear a plain colour shirt and trousers when going ashore so as not to draw attention to myself, but it is difficult to get it right sometimes. In the Caribbean I show up because I am a white person in a mainly black community, but everywhere in the world cruise passengers always look different. Their sunhats are seldom from the country they are in so you see baseball caps with 'Bermuda' emblazoned on their fronts in Africa and 'Greenland' on a favourite cap worn regularly to protect the scalp from the sun. Blending in is impossible because the locals all know when a ship is in. They can't wait to sell you all the souvenirs you thought you couldn't live without until you get them home. For me, there is also the guilt factor. I am so lucky, so much wealthier than them. I meet their mournful, pleading eyes and find myself buying wooden necklaces I will never wear and packets of strange spices to store forgotten with all the others in my kitchen.

Although I'm usually happy enough to spend a morning on my own, on one occasion I was pleased to hear a voice call, "Are you on your tod, love? Come with us if you like." I paused and turned round, clinging to my bag as people pushed past. After fighting my way through hoards of faces, all exhorting me, "Lady, lady, you follow me, you buy?" it was a relief to hear a familiar Irish voice. Brenda and Jake and their friends are fun, and as the Doc was working all day it'd be good to have company. We were on Nosy Be, the largest island of Madagascar. It's known as 'L'ile Parfumee' the perfumed island, because it grows ylang-ylang, lemongrass, patchouli, vanilla, sugar cane, cinnamon, coffee, pepper and saffron.

Within minutes, Jake had acquired one of the few air-conditioned taxis on the island and we set off. We stopped for a short time in Andoany or 'Hell-Ville', the capital of the island. "Will you go round the market with me?" I asked Brenda, feeling a little ruffled as I got jostled by a group of passing youths. This was not a place to wander round on your own. Inside the huge, dark warehouse, there were small wooden stalls piled one upon another, all seemingly selling the same fruit and vegetables. In one corner, an African housewife was examining piles of fly-ridden meat, her forehead shiny with sweat, and I pushed past to plunge my nose into a stall full of herbs, breathing in their pleasant scent. The women looked after the stalls but there were men in the background waiting to argue and bully customers into buying. Because of this I didn't stay and ask about the meat and how it would be cooked, and the man who sold me some herbs was scowling and unhelpful because I only wanted a small amount. After the chaos inside it was a relief to see our taxi man waving from across the street when we emerged into the sunlight. From the safe confines of his taxi, every building resembled a battered ruin about to collapse and our exasperated driver thumbed his horn angrily at the emaciated dogs rooting in piles of garbage in the road. If it were not for his wealthy passengers, I am sure he would simply run over them. Other obstacles, cows pulling carts, ancient cars, buses and scooters, competed to swell the noise and everywhere there were crowds of people, milling around the stalls and spilling out onto the streets. We compared notes in the back seat and decided that 'Hell-Ville,' was aptly named.

The countryside was a much sweeter place. We travelled slowly over roads full of potholes, swerving to avoid ducks, goats, chickens and small children who smiled and waved on their way to school. Their homes were tiny wooden huts in grassy enclosures at the side of the road. Some of them were circular, with roofs thatched with bamboo leaves. We passed small plantations of ylang-ylang, peculiar trees that seemed to have their roots in the air and leaves and branches on the ground. We paused to pick coffee berries and pepper and passed through fields of sugar cane way above our heads. "Stop, stop," I begged the driver for the third time. Beside a balloon shaped house with a thatched roof, a small boy was holding up a lemur for us to see. Its huge, panda-like eyes, edged with black fur, stared mournfully at me from the arms of its diminutive owner. I handed over one American dollar for a photograph and laughed as all his small relations suddenly appeared from nowhere. They carried tiny bottles of yellow perfume and we hastily produced a few more dollars before making our escape.

A bit further on, the road disappeared altogether and we climbed a long muddy track on foot to the summit of Mount Passot, the island's highest point. The sight of the long string of crater lakes below us made Brenda feel like a swim. "Let's ask him to take us to the beach," she suggested. Nosey Be is a French-speaking island and I was delegated to discuss this with the taxi-driver. "La plage, s'il vous plait?" I asked in my schoolgirl French. He looked surprised. We were in the centre of the island and at the top of a mountain after all. Then he shrugged and nodded and we were off again, bumping and bouncing over the road.

The Indian Ocean was just like a warm bath and I felt distinctly decadent as we lolled in knee-deep water, relaxing with cans of cola bought from the wooden shack on the beach. Today there were no sea urchins, sting rays or other nasty creatures waiting to prey on us in the sea but, as the afternoon progressed, taxis disgorged more and more passengers from the ship until the beach looked like a kind of select club, with group meetings and friendly games going on all over it. Word of our invasion spread and soon local people arrived on foot out of the forest, laden with tee-shirts, necklaces, perfume, and woodcarvings to sell.

We lingered too long and our taxi driver was nowhere to be seen when we left the beach. Eventually, he was discovered, fast asleep in the bushes, his mouth wide open. We were anxious not to miss the last tender but there was even more traffic on the road, processions of people strolling home from work in the fields, and animals and children who wandered aimlessly along in the evening sunlight.

When we eventually returned to the small quay, prices had dropped. Balsa wood aeroplanes were selling for a few dollars and bags of mangoes were thrust aboard the tender with cries of "one dollar, only one dollar," while the harassed crew tried to cast off. Back on board, clutching too many bottles of ylang-ylang oil, I found the Doc and presented him with a tee-shirt decorated with seven lemurs. "Had a good day?" he asked.

" I've been from hell to paradise," I replied.

That evening we were besieged by a large number of small dug-out canoes that surrounded our ship. The little outriggers were full of smiling family groups waving as they brandished bags of fresh fruit and wooden carvings above their heads. Down in the crew area on Deck 3, the Doc fancied a lovely carved tortoise about the size of a melon and some crew-members showed him how to buy it. You placed a ten-dollar bill in a plastic bag, tied the top firmly and lowered it on a piece of string over the side of the ship. The relevant boat below moved in, the owner took the money and tied your purchase on to the string so it could be slowly brought up on board. There was a great deal of pointing and head shaking involved with seemingly no problems. This was a crew-only enterprise while the passengers looked on from the upper decks and took photographs.There was no evidence of cheating or being cheated. The crew had obviously been to the island before and both they and the locals enjoyed this lucrative retail system. It gave a new meaning to 'shopping online'.

So far we have been lucky on our travels and have only been 'nearly' robbed twice, a wallet 'almost' neatly removed from the Doc's trousers on the crowded metro in Barcelona and in St Petersburg, a rucksack, neatly opened from behind. "There they go, we saw them," shouted the two men behind us, but later we realised that they themselves had been the ones attempting to rob us. Now I wear a soft bag around my waist with only a small amount of money in it. If I need to carry a credit card, I put it in my shoe between two pairs of socks. The Doc carries a purse around his neck hidden under a shirt. Removing this purse to get at the money involves a few contortions, especially when several layers are concerned, but it feels safer.

People who look around at the architecture while walking in the street are not being streetwise. Locals know what's there so they never look at anything. Trying to do this while surreptitiously surveying the scenery gives me a headache and makes me go cross-eyed, so I have abandoned it. I just look like a starry-eyed tourist who trusts in the goodness of everyone around me and usually I'm all right.

A whole book could be written about taxi travel around the world. Because we leave the ship later than the passengers, we frequently take a taxi to see the sights, but negotiating the fare, the length and the itinerary is a serious business. We have learnt to write down the agreed price before getting in the taxi while allowing for a slight detour here and there (usually to "my brother's shop – not very far"). If we are lucky we get a kind, enthusiastic driver who tells us about his country as he drives us to all the most interesting places. We might get a boat trip thrown in, or a local lunch or even a visit to his home to meet the family. The one golden rule is never to pay all of the fare before you are safely returned to base. I was once almost abandoned with a friend on a lonely beach in Dominica, but I had insisted on paying afterwards. Waiting anxiously on a lonely road, and at least half an hour late, a battered old car drew up with our driver in it. "Where's your taxi?" we asked.

"Not mine, madam, it had to go back. I rent it for a few hours a day." He had walked home to get his own car to come and collect us, and the money of course.

Once, flushed with success after a visit to the carpet souk in Istanbul, we piled our shopping purchases into a taxi to return to the cruise terminal. My friend Joy had successfully bargained for a rug and we enthused about her skills as we drove all over the city streets. The agreed fare was ten dollars and I handed it over quickly as the car stopped outside the port. Unknown to us this unlicensed taxi was not allowed inside so we would have to walk the rest of the way.

"You have only give me one dollar," the man protested, holding it aloft.

"Oh, sorry," I replied, looking more closely at the note this time. But he tried the same trick again.

"This also, only one dollar." But I wasn't falling for that.

"You now have twenty one dollars and we don't have any more," I replied forcefully, and we hastily scrambled out, ignoring his protests about poverty and the government. Once back on board ship we compared notes with other passengers and were pleased when our deal with the wily taxi man seemed to have been more reasonable than some people who had paid a great deal more, but really we were just relieved to have safely returned with our purchases.

A Short Visit to Kenya

Sometimes the sad duties associated with repatriating a sick passenger become more important than trying to keep them on board. On this occasion the medical team were involved in sending Maria home because, despite all their efforts, she was simply not well enough to continue the cruise. Transport, flights, escorts and medication had to be arranged and checked so I volunteered to look after myself in Mombasa.

"Don't wander round here on your own," I was warned by the security officer, so I joined an afternoon beach tour from the ship. As the coach dawdled in the traffic queues through streets mired in unbelievable squalor, it was an education to look down on piles of rubbish lying in the streets. Babies played in piles of vegetables, while bare-footed women with baskets on their heads moved gingerly past small engineering businesses, as they tried to avoid the oily remnants of cars and rusty metal spilling from their tin sheds on to the pavement. This made them lethal to walk on, with the added hazards of broken cement slabs and uncovered drains. When forced to walk in the road, I could see that pedestrians often had to jump for their lives as impatient drivers plunged on to the edge of the pavement to try to overtake on the inside.

Our destination, Nyana Beach Hotel, on the outskirts

of the city, was in quite a different area, with imposing mansions whose wide, shady streets were lined with flowering trees. As we drove into the hotel entrance, smart men in white suits leapt to greet us. My companion, an experienced, long-term cruiser, marched forward into the lobby and was quickly able to obtain two sun loungers by the hotel pool for us. With a flash of a crisp dollar bill they were moved into the shade with a view of the sea in front. Ignoring the pool, I went off for my first swim in the Indian Ocean but the murky water revealed slimy weeds that attached themselves to my ankles, so I changed my mind and went back to the highly chlorinated pool.

Even a few lengths of lazy breast stroke is thirsty work, but buying drinks from the beach bar took longer than expected: my lack of local currency flustered the barman but I was determined to get us a drink somehow. After a long mathematical discussion that was getting us nowhere, I persuaded him to accept my dollar bills but, although he provided ice for the coke, when we tasted our drinks we both thought he had been a bit sparing with the Bacardi!

The next day, I was able to be the escort for the ship's Mombasa city tour. I was pleased because it would be a safe way of seeing some more of this interesting city. On our way from the port along Moi Avenue, we passed the Mombasa Tusks, an archway of two crossed elephant tusks made out of sheet metal, erected to commemorate Queen Elizabeth's visit in 1952.

Our first destination was the Akamba Woodcarving Factory, a maze of small wooden huts employing three thousand people. Every one of the skilled male carvers spends his whole life making just one object: a giraffe, lion or other animal or maybe carving an African Chieftain's head. The men sat cross-legged on the floor with wood shavings piling up around them and then polished the finished items with Kiwi shoe polish.

I was worried that I would lose someone at our next stop, when we formed a long line to walk through a maze of passages lined with stalls. We struggled through the crowds of shoppers to a spice shop in the middle of a busy market. "Everything that's past its sell by date from all over the world must end up here," I thought as I steered two errant wanderers in the right direction. In the open-fronted shop, sacks of spices mingled with boxes of what looked like dried fruits and vegetables but I couldn't identify many of them. Behind them the walls were lined with jars of herbs and medicinal preparations. The owner, a harassed African in a grubby white coat, was trying to give us a talk on their contents but voluble customers kept pushing in and demanding his attention so he gave up with a shake of his head. I bought a packet of ground coffee and was relieved to find that, on my return to the bus, everyone else had arrived back safely too.

Another walk followed, this time into the old town, which still showed signs of its ancient Swahili heritage. There were no crowds here so I was able to look upwards at the white misshapen walls that curved around corners of narrow alleys. Doors and shutters had intricately carved designs and I took some photos to show the Doc. Unfortunately looking up turned out not to be such a good idea. There was an open drain in the middle of our path containing a dead rat and tons of rotting vegetables and small bits of something slimy got wedged under my toes. We finally emerged on a wide road leading to Fort Jesus. The Portuguese built this fort as the main hub for trading goods during their two hundred year reign over

Mombasa. It was also used as a prison. There were cells and torture rooms inside that had formerly held slaves, before they were sold to European trading ships in exchange for spices, cotton and coffee. Nearby, there was a town bell that had originally been used to warn locals to run and hide from the slave-catchers who were coming to get them.

On our last day in Mombasa the Doc and I booked a whole day tour to Tsavo National Park. A new doctor had arrived from the UK and was 'on call' for the day so we were free. We left the ship at 6.30am armed with sun cream, hats and cameras, travelling in minibuses with roofs that could be pushed up so that we could view the game when we arrived at the park. We drove on the main road between Mombasa to Nairobi, part of which was being rebuilt. At the time we were on it the new road was not completed and so we travelled on the old road that ran parallel to it. We soon recognised the relevance of a large sign that read 'Stop Corruption, Build our Road.' There were six of us in each bus and it was a very uncomfortable journey! The road was so potholed that we had to strap ourselves in to stay put and avoid hitting the roof as we bounced along. Our driver, perhaps fortuitously named Jesus, spoke excellent English and cheerfully assured everyone that the minibus was used to bumps. In places the road surface was simply dry mud and, even with the windows closed, the dust poured in and turned our faces yellow. No air-conditioning meant that sometimes we simply had to open the windows to cool us down and we drank frequently from the bottles of water supplied by Jesus. By the time we got there I was wishing he could have turned it into wine because everyone was feeling shaken up. However, we were fortunate compared to the women walking by on the road with water pots on their heads. I watched as they collected muddy, brown water from ditches. Other women came out of the bush to get charcoal for fuel, which was left by the side of the road. In the distance we could see the small missionary villages where they lived, a circle of small dwellings surrounding a church.

Inside the Park, the safari tracks seemed quite comfortable in comparison and we soon recovered when the roof was extended and we began a slow amble across the plain with binoculars at the ready. Antelope, warthogs and a giraffe ignored us and secretary birds with very long legs ran along in front scolding in a loud voice. Round a corner we found a large family group of elephants sheltering under a tree. Jesus kept up a frequent dialogue on his walkie-talkie with drivers in other minibuses who told him where to go for the next best game-viewing area. Often, when we arrived, there were other buses jostling for the best space and on board we took turns to take photos and game-gaze.

During lunch at the Voi Safari Lodge, we were amused by the antics of baboons swinging above our heads, hoping to snatch food scraps if they could avoid being chased off by the waiters. Hyrax (small squirrel-like animals but without the bushy tail) and multi-coloured geckos sunned themselves on the low garden walls on which we leaned. Below us on the plain, herds of elephant grazed peacefully. I loved the impala with their delicate legs, the chunky wildebeest and a strange animal that looked like a cross between a giraffe and an antelope. It was known as a Gerenuk and had the body of an antelope with an extraordinary long neck and small head. We saw several trying to climb into the trees using their front legs to balance against the trunk while plunging their long necks into the higher branches.

The return journey to the ship was even more horrendous than the first. Weaving and juddering from left to right to miss the biggest pits, we came to a place where the road we had used in the morning had been closed and a deep trench dug across it. Huge lorries lined up on each side and our driver finally took off into the bush to find a way around, with his mobile phone clamped to his ear all the while! When we finally got back on the road after driving over a kind of giant sandbank, it was to find another traffic jam. Surrounded by lorries, cars, people, goats, dogs, children and dust we opened our last bottles of water and prepared for a long wait while a few hundred spectators watched in anticipation. Fortunately, after a while, the police came along. My eyes were popping out of my head when I saw the big guns they carried. Waving them importantly, they made a way through for all our tourist buses, bullying other vehicles into the side.

In the end, we were only two hours late getting back to the ship but our sailing was delayed for several hours for other reasons. At the top of the gangway, the Doc was immediately summoned to the medical centre where several emergencies had arrived all at once. A sun umbrella had knocked out one passenger, another had a severe diabetic problem and a third had suffered a stroke. With only time for a quick change into uniform and still looking suspiciously yellow, he rushed down to the medical centre to help deal with all the problems.

The next morning, our last in Kenya, I went ashore to browse among the stalls on the dockside. I hadn't had time to buy anything over the last few days except the coffee, but I had a good idea of what I would like if I could find it. A long line of sellers, their goods spread out on the ground, reached from one end of the quay to the other. The walls of the wooden warehouses behind them were used to hang haphazard collections of clothes, paintings and material. I quickly learned that prices were cheaper on the stalls furthest away from the gangway and the most enterprising passengers stayed on board with their binoculars, checking out their choice of goods before going down to bargain for them. The initial price is never the price to pay. You must laugh at it in amazement and then offer two thirds lower. The smiling African seller will then ridicule your suggestion and there follows a mental ballet of ups and downs until a satisfactory compromise is reached. If you manage to stay calm (and I never do), the eventual price is usually one third of the original. I walked up and down several times in a disinterested manner that fooled nobody. Then, with a long list in my head and a frantic wave to the upper deck, I called upon the Medical Officer to come and buy for me. The Doc is very good at bartering but I cringed at his brisk, 'take it or leave it' manner as he dragged me away empty-handed, only to be called back immediately. After several exhausting encounters like this I was ready to give up and not buy anything at all. But he stayed firm and soon I was lucky and found myself hurrying up the gangway, carrying crumpled carrier bags full of news-wrapped souvenirs of Africa to take home.

Breakfast on Deck

The nicest thing about being 'crew's wife' is getting to know some of the interesting people who work on board. Friendships blossom and die and in between our cruise contracts anything can happen. Because I am seldom on board long enough to find out the true ending to these fairytale romances my imagination can work overtime!

Our nurses are a wonderful mix of both nationalities and personalities. They all have one thing in common and that is their professionalism and experience. There are usually two permanent Nursing Officers who alternate duties and sometimes a third nurse from the Philippines. There are also agency nurses who fill in from time to time. They never seemed to mind having different doctors for every cruise and quickly assimilate them into clinic routines.

On one cruise we had a particularly attractive nurse. Bubbly and energetic she bounced around the ship attracting the attention of a handsome Norwegian officer. They fell in love and life in the medical centre changed dramatically. Every morning before clinic her voice could be heard chatting confidentially on the phone. "Hello Ducky, how are you? Are you having a good day?" The first time the startled Doc heard this he thought the remarks were directed at him but soon realised his mistake. As soon as clinic was finished and sometimes before, in would come the object of her affection on the pretext of some technical problem or other. He would wander restlessly around the medical centre until the coast was clear and they could sit and make eyes at one another over a cup of coffee collected from the crew mess. At night, barring emergencies of course, there was no sign of either of them and we were all left guessing until a casual remark one day gave the game away. Nora, a nursing colleague, had bought a collection of souvenirs she was intending to take home eventually. Complaining that she had run out of space in her cabin her friend said airily. "Don't worry, you can put it in mine. I'm not using it at the moment." Obviously things were getting serious but as long as work was not affected the Doc said nothing, especially as requests by the Medical Centre were suddenly being met with a favourable response from on high and the glow of their happiness seemed to rub off on all of us. However, sadly, as the affair progressed, the lovelorn couple must have overstepped the mark somewhere and much to my private frustration, before our next cruise they had both been dismissed for reasons no one was willing to divulge.

Many officers are Norwegian, though there are also some from Poland, Germany and other European countries. One of the housekeeping officers had a fearsome reputation for his strict adherence to the rules. Much like his height and upright demeanour he made no allowances for any deviations and word got round quickly when it was seen that he had arrived on board. He seemed to have a knack of turning up and catching the nurses and entertainment staff unawares just as they had settled in a small corner of a bar for a gossip and a quiet drink. There was a rule, seldom applied, that junior officers should only be seen together in twos and Johan would swiftly disperse larger groups, who would separate muttering indignantly still clutching their glasses.

I had become friendly with one of the nurses, Henrietta, or Henny as she was called, and one evening she joined me on the balcony of the Neptune Lounge to watch the performance. Tired after being on her feet all day she was sitting down next to me. Officers are not supposed to sit when in the company of passengers and I soon noticed the looming bulk of Johan approaching. "You are not allowed to sit while on duty Nurse," he rumbled in her ear.

Henny's one word reply was fortunately buried in a blast of trumpet music from the orchestra, but his intervention seemed petty and unnecessary when there were empty spaces all around us. Fortunately, the Doc had chosen to stay near the entrance so that he could hear the bleep if it went off, otherwise he might well have been sitting down too!

From then on it was open warfare between Henny and Johan, though to me as an amused bystander, it was more like the attraction of opposites. Henny was determined not to be intimidated by this huge six foot Norwegian who seemed to have an aversion to female officers and, for some reason, to her in particular. "It's sexual prejudice," she muttered to me. Some of the Norwegian officers, in particular, did appear to treat women officers as inferior to their male counterparts but I felt this was sometimes due to their working conditions on board rather than discrimination. The Officers' mess was mainly used for meals and there was seldom time for social chit-chat. Every morning when she went to breakfast Henny marched up to Johan. "Good Morning," she said loudly, forcing him to respond to her greeting. This was no mean feat given that he rarely spoke to any woman except, it seemed, for rule reminders. Afterwards, all of four foot ten with curly hair and freckles, Henny would flounce into morning clinic to regale everyone with the latest instalment of Johan responses. The day became a game of cat-and-mouse and she never missed an opportunity to pounce on Johan with some complaint or other whenever he appeared. Any small matter that could be deemed to apply to 'housekeeping' she took to him. By the end of the cruise he was studiously avoiding her and the nurses could relax a little. To be honest, the Doc and I got used to the dour Norwegian and gradually became almost friends. Now and again he would divulge a little of his home life and might even break into a smile if mildly amused by one of the Doc's tales. It must be said that despite his abrupt manner, the housekeeping department always ran smoothly while he was on board.

I loved the warm parts of the world like the Caribbean, when I would often have breakfast on deck on my own. On one particular morning on the return leg of a cruise to the Amazon, fresh pineapple and a bacon sandwich went down very well in the sunshine while I thought about what to do today in Bridgetown, Barbados. It was early and not many passengers were up yet but I didn't mind my own company. My feet tapped the deck to the sound of the steel band playing on the quay and a wobbly pelican flew lazily overhead doing a spot of morning fishing. They are ungainly birds in flight but can dive for fish with amazing accuracy spearing their prey on long sharp beaks.

This time of the morning is a good time to meet other people who are on their own, but it's not always pleasurable. Today Pamela joined me; she was a large lady from somewhere in the South of England who told me this was her third solo cruise. We discussed Panama hats and how to travel with them. She had packed hers in her luggage, filling the brim with rolled up nylon tights while I carried mine in a plastic bag so it wouldn't get squashed. Unfortunately a Chinese student put his rucksack on top of it on the plane so it will never be quite the same. I could see I should never wear it again. It's either too windy or too rainy at home and now it's flattened. I also had a white cotton hat I dropped and stood on the day before. Pamela was sympathetic and suggested I visit the ship's boutique for a replacement. It's always slightly awkward at the beginning of a conversation because inevitably the question, "Are you travelling alone?" arises. I then have to decide either to tell a lie such as, "My husband is still asleep," or, "He's walking around somewhere," (accompanied by an airy wave of the hand and a glance around to see if I can find him) or offer a firm "No" without any explanation. Rarely do I admit at this stage that he is the ship's medical officer. In the worst case scenario my companion might fix me with a glittering eye and pour forth a usually disastrous medical history and my breakfast and my peace of mind are spoilt. Not everyone responds like this, of course, but sadly there are some who think that the one subject of interest to anyone involved in the medical profession is their own personal heart, bowel, gynaecological, surgical or any other health problems.

Gradually, as I became a more confident cruiser, I learned a few new techniques. I bought a hat with a large brim and strap to keep it on and also wore sunglasses. I took a book and opened it beside my coffee cup so I could appear to be reading if I suspected unwanted company was hovering. Then, in case I caught sight of a likely kindred spirit, I would be able to whip off the glasses and welcome them to join me.

One such was a cheerful man called Tony. We had passed the time of day a few times in the corridor on the way to our respective cabins. Knowing I'm married to the Doc he joined me occasionally for breakfast probably realising, quite rightly, there were no strings attached to my company. Men travelling alone are prone to find they are in great demand on board ship, especially on the long days at sea, so on this cruise we seem to have ended up with this mutually satisfactory breakfast arrangement. I seldom saw him at other times of the day.

We had been to Australia and Tony was travelling from Sydney. He said he would leave the ship soon and was to fly to America to do a six-month course to learn how to become a blacksmith. This might have been a fantasy statement, of course, and I made no comment on it. Many new lives are created on board a cruise ship. Other than that I knew little else about him, though it was rumoured he left a girlfriend in Australia. He enjoyed telling me about the local on-board gossip. That morning it was about one woman whose behaviour had scandalised some matronly female passengers. The previous evening she had joined the late night dancing on deck wearing very little in the way of underwear, or rather 'no knickers', said Tony with obvious relish. I realised that I had noticed the lady in question before and rather admired her slinky leopard-skin mini-dress and long auburn hair. She looked much younger than me from my position behind her in the queue for afternoon tea, but when she turned round I realised that with our mutually lined faces, we were probably of a similar age. I was dying to ask Tony whether she was in fact wearing a thong but decided not to get in any deeper!

The next morning, over coffee and croissants, Tony told me the next instalment in his tale of our mystery flasher. He had managed to invade her group for evening drinks and found out that she was travelling with her husband and that she owned a brothel in Australia. “Well, fancy that,” I murmured, unable to think of a more sensible reply. Secretly I rather admired the courage of her flamboyant behaviour but felt I needed to adhere to my respectable ‘doctor’s wife’ reputation. At the same time I must say I was enjoying the steely glances from a group of ladies at the next table who, seeing me with my suntanned companion, were obviously putting two and two together and making five!

The last time I saw the bold brothel owner we were in the airport lounge in Hawaii. In the inevitable queue in the ladies’ toilets she was in front of me. A moment later that same mini dress was flung on top of the cubicle door. Then she emerged wearing jeans and warm jacket just like the rest of us, all ready for the cooler climate in Vancouver, our next stop on the journey home.

The Horn and Highlights of Chile

One of the attractions of a cruise to South America is going 'Round the Horn'. All the way from Rio de Janeiro where we had joined the ship, and then visiting exciting places like Montevideo in Uruguay, Buenos Aires in Argentina and Port Stanley in the Falklands, I had been looking forward to going round the Horn. Tales of terrible weather, howling gales and sunken ships were ingrained in my memory from long ago history lessons. Summoned to the decks by the loudspeakers at 8am, I found passengers shivering in anticipation in the cold morning mist. A chill breeze stirred the air and sent me scuttling to shelter behind the sun deck's Perspex window as we waited, cameras poised for the moment! An announcement from the bridge informed us that the hump of land on the starboard side was Cape Horn. As we came in closer to shore, it looked slightly more impressive and I leaned on the rail to take photos of the black piece of rock jutting out to sea and the jagged boulders beneath it, knowing in my heart that I was not likely to ever see it again. Actually I was wrong about that, because the ship went past Cape Horn, out to sea a little, then turned round and went past it again before entering the Beagle Channel. This strait separates the islands of Tierra del Fuego, near the southernmost tip of South America. The western part of the channel is in

Chile, and the eastern part forms a boundary between Argentina to the North and Chile to the south. The channel is named after HMS Beagle, Charles Darwin's vessel, which surveyed it during his journey round the world between 1831 and 1836. Today with mild seas and little wind to rock our modern cruise ship, going round the Horn was not the romantic moment I had imagined, so feeling cold and damp and more than a little disappointed I went below to find hot porridge for breakfast.

Ushuiaia is at the foot of the Martial Mountains and was the biggest settlement on the Eastern side of the Beagle Channel. It was also the capital of Southern Argentina and was for many years a penal colony. To me it appeared to be so far away from anywhere that it seemed a good place to send all the people labelled criminals so that you never had to think of them again. Reinforcing this idea as we docked was a huge sign saying: 'Welcome to the Port of World's End,' in English and Spanish.

Nowadays ships sail south from here to the Antarctic. The tourist quay has a bustling holiday atmosphere designed to entice cruise passengers, but there seemed little relevance to Patagonian life: Painted clowns, Indians in full costume, a large person dressed as a penguin and a lone tango dancer shivering in the icy breeze were waiting to welcome us ashore.

As usual, the Doc was busy on board so I joined a three-hour escorted walk through the Tierra del Fuego National Park. Our guide, Iris, with a degree in Ecology and Tourism, had an extensive knowledge of the plants and trees around us. She maintained a fast pace and it was quite difficult trying to keep up, study the scenery and not trip over the huge roots across the path. Once or twice she stopped suddenly and we all cannoned into each other in a breathless scrum. There was a great deal to see. The beautiful trees, mainly Southern Beech trees, were home to unusual birds. Giant Magellan woodpeckers high above us drilled the bark, ignoring our passage below. Sea birds pottered with their young on the shoreline. We also saw a red fox that was as curious about us as we were about it. It watched warily while we took photos and then trotted off. At the end of the walk we came to a landing jetty and boarded a Zodiac inflatable boat. It took us on a bumpy ride to a small island in the middle of the channel. Our lunch was set out in a hut above another rickety landing stage. Inside, we sat at a long trestle table with a rusty wood-burner at one end and ate spaghetti bolognese washed down with red wine. The combination of wood-burner and wine warmed me so much that afterwards I was glad to sit outside in the mild sunlight and nibble chocolate cake until it was time to rejoin the boat and motor up the channel to Latapaia, where our tour bus was waiting. We travelled through suburbs of wooden houses all of different designs and colours. The guide spoke very loudly into the microphone to make sure we heard her commentary: "In the eighties, people coming to live in this area were given money to build houses but they were not allowed to buy the land. They built their homes on platforms that could be moved somewhere else if necessary."

After the tour there was just time to pick up my emails from a small café. One message from my friend in our village said, "Yesterday was show day. I won first prize for my home made sponge and for once I beat Mrs Deacon. I'll freeze a bit for you for when you come home." It left me feeling a bit homesick.

Outside the port entrance I offered my remaining Argentine pesos to a young man dressed as a clown who was sitting on a step with two girls in national costume.As I moved away he called to me and I heard footsteps running from behind. He offered me a photo of himself as a souvenir, and gave me a big kiss on the cheek. I went back to the ship with a big red blob on my face but it cheered me up. Perhaps Ushuaia was not so bad after all.

The next day, we were fjord-watching from the warmth of the observatory lounge when we suddenly noticed that the ship's engines had stopped and that tenders were being lowered. Not an emergency, the Captain reassured us. It was just a little side trip to brighten the day organised by the ship's owner who was on board. Those who didn't mind wrapping up warmly were led down the gangway and into the waiting boats and I quickly joined the queue. We set off for the Amalia glacier, a twenty-minute boat ride away, through water as smooth as glass. I looked back to see the steep sides of the fjord perfectly mirrored in its depths. Glacial water is always a different colour from that of other lakes and this water was a milky blue, like the ice wall that came into view in front of us. It was as if a wide torrent of water had frozen solid in the very act of tumbling down the mountain into the lake. Beyond it the path of ice meandered round the cone of an extinct volcano. Nowadays it is in retreat we were told, but from the viewpoint of our small lifeboat, it resembled a formidable cliff towering over us. The crew nudged the boat in as close to it as possible and leaned over the side with axes to chip off chunks of ice. The ice blocks floated free in the freezing water and we all cheered when with a few boat manoeuvres, they were finally scooped up on board and put in large plastic sacks. Back on board ship, we were presented, like returning heroes, with a tot of whisky in which floated ice from the three thousand year old glacier.

A complete change of temperature faced us when we reached the north of Chile. Arica is the most northern city and sits on the edge of the Atacama Desert. It faces the coast with mountainous dunes behind. They were not like the sand dunes we saw in Namibia on another cruise, which were golden and soft. These were gritty, yellow-grey mountains, that seldom got washed since it rarely rained until you got to the Altiplano, the Highlands where there was enough rain to allow animals to be raised on the tough grass. The Doc was free so we negotiated with a taxi driver to take us to see some geoglyphs. These are ancient pictures in stones high up on the sides of the dunes, depicting llamas, birds and people with their arms spread out like wings. There were other patterns too that I did not recognise. They can be found all over the desert and are believed to be near ancient track ways, perhaps acting as signposts along a llama transportation route, long before there were any roads. Our driver couldn't speak much English but he waited patiently while we got out and photographed the strange pictures in the sand mountains. Further on we drove through a fertile region with olive plantations on either side of the road and walled haciendas that seemed to be mainly fruit-growing businesses. There were a few people working on them; we saw someone spraying tomatoes and hoeing the stony ground between the plants. There were a great many mango trees, their branches bent low with ripe fruit, and also paw paws and avocados. We stopped the taxi again at the entrance to a golf club, and the Doc, a keen golfer, went off to explore the extraordinary sight of smooth mountains of dry sand, with compressed black sand where the greens should be. From the road you only knew they were greens because of the flags in the holes. The only green colour around was provided by a couple of palm trees in the courtyard of the clubhouse. Being slightly nervous that the driver might drive away with me and leave the Doc behind, I got out smiling apologetically and stood beside the taxi. For a few moments I felt vulnerable and very small, standing on the empty road. Lack of a mutual language makes ordinary conversation impossible and there were only so many smiles and signs you could make when standing on opposite sides of a car. It was quite a relief when the Doc returned and we resumed our journey.

Further on we drove through olive plantations, but strangely we did not see any streams or irrigation ditches like those we had seen in other dry areas of the world. My guidebook stated that the Atacama Desert has little or no rainfall and is known as the driest place on earth. Farmers water their crops with drip irrigation systems, collecting scarce water from underground aquifers which perhaps explained the lack of surface water.

The museum of St Miguel , our eventual destination, was a small insignificant building. We stood in the shade of its walls while the taxi-driver bought us drinks from a wooden kiosk and we drank thirstily from the bottles. Inside the museum, spread out on large tables, lay the real reason for our journey, the sand mummies: thought to be of a tribe known as Chinchorros, they were displayed on padded tables, two brown, wrinkled adults of small stature and a tiny baby. Their bodies had been completely dismembered and then reassembled with all but the bones and skin replaced by clay, reeds and various other stuffing materials. A mask of clay with small incisions for the eyes and mouth, was placed on their faces. It was supposed to give the impression of peaceful slumber but to me it seemed to give them a mysterious persona, as if under the mask their spirits were watching us. They had been found with items of wool and ceramics under building excavations near Arica, preserved by the sand and dry climate and dating from before 1000BC.

No one seemed to know why the Chinchorros preserved their dead in this way, though the condition of similar bodies found in other areas of Chile suggested they had not all been buried but carried around for ritual celebrations and worship. This seemed very gruesome to me until the Doc reminded me of a day out to distribute his Uncle's ashes. "Remember Uncle Jack," he said. We'd put the funeral urn in a rucksack and walked to the top of a hill to scatter them in his favourite places, as he had requested. Perhaps our cultures were not so very different after all. We enjoyed this half hour in the museum that gave us the chance to ponder on earlier lives so different from our own. There was no-one else there and no sound except for the buzzing of a few insects hitting the wired window frames. Outside, our courteous driver shuffled his feet as he smoked a cigarette, perhaps letting us know it was time to go. On the return journey, after a short exchange of sign language and head nodding, he took a short diversion so that we could buy delicious, ripe mangoes from a wooden stall by the side of the road.

Machu Picchu

Instead of flying directly home after one cruise we joined a group of ship's passengers for a four-day tour. The Doc was quite euphoric as we boarded the plane for the one-hour flight to Cuzco. No more morning clinics and lingering problems to worry about. There were forty-two of us including Jeremy, our ship's representative and Nevers, the guide from the local travel company. We had been warned about altitude sickness but took little notice. I vaguely thought it was something like seasickness, which I had quickly learned to control a long time ago, so it was a shock to arrive in Cuzco and find that I immediately felt unwell when we left the plane. I turned the other way when a photographer tried to take my photo so he caught the Doc instead and was soon busily touting for business among the others. By the time we reached the hotel, I was exhausted and could feel my heart pounding. I flopped into a comfortable settee in the reception area and sipped gratefully at the small cup of coca tea offered to me. It is supposed to be good for altitude sickness but it tasted of very little really, just like weak, milk-less tea. Anyway there was no time to dwell on one's health. We were given half an hour to take our cases to our rooms and then we were off for the day's explorations by coach. At the hotel entrance small children besieged us selling all kinds of things. "Remember me, I'm number one," one little boy called after me brandishing his shoeshine kit. "When you come back, lady?" There seemed to be hundreds of children but the guide explained that today was a school holiday. Normally, the children went to school in the morning, the afternoon or the evening, and in between they worked.

The streets of Cuzco were lined with low buildings made of mud bricks, although there were grander buildings on the main street leading to the Square. These were little local shops where people cluttered up the doorways or sat propped up against the walls outside. Bowler-hatted women, some wearing three hats one on top of the other, and in national costume of brightly-coloured skirts and black short jackets, strode purposefully past waiting to accost hapless tourists like us.

The bus drove first to the sacred valley of the Incas. We stopped and took photos of the valley with three thin little Peruvian girls in national costume to give our pictures colour. Although brightly dressed, their faces were pale and they looked undernourished. We bought strange pottery whistles from them as payment for our photos. In the small colourful town of Pisac, our guide, Juan Carlos, took us on a walking tour of the market, pointing out different fruits and vegetables and warning us not to eat anything offered to us because it was not washed. His cries of "Dear Guests" and "My Lady" when he addressed one of the women became a popular and familiar part of our tour as the day went on. We lunched in the garden of what looked like a former monastery. It still had its bell tower and arched doorways but inside it was more like a traditional Spanish estancia with long tables and benches and walls decorated with whips and leather horse tackle. The buffet was designed to attract our appetites but I still felt strangely apathetic and could only manage a small portion of salad and bread. Apparently this is a side effect of the altitude. I couldn't help feeling that if we stayed long enough maybe it would make a good aid to losing weight after a long, self-indulgent cruise. A couple of llamas grazed peacefully on the lawn with chickens and ducks getting under their feet until a kick from a powerful hoof sent one hen skittering off squawking loudly.

Just before we got back on the coach again, the airport photographer arrived and I bought a card with a rather over-exposed Doc on it. Having been 'snapped' when he got off the plane, his picture was developed, and stuck on a postcard of Cuzco. This enterprising man had followed us out here to sell his pictures and did quite well, as everyone wanted a photo /postcard of themselves. A short rest in the coach revived me and I was able to join the Doc at our next stop and climb the steep steps at the Inca fortress of Ollantaytambo that zigzagged upwards to the Temple of the Sun. There is a legend attached to these ruins about the Inca captain Ollanta. He fell in love with the daughter of Pachacutec, the reigning monarch at the time. As they were not allowed to marry, Ollanta kidnapped the princess and took her to his fortress. In the battle that followed, Pachacutec was killed, but Ollanta was betrayed before he could take control of the empire. Eventually the new Inca ruler, recognising that he was a good warrior, allowed him to marry and he and his bride lived out their lives in Ollantaytambo. In historical Spanish records the story is not so romantic. The fortress became the retreat of Manco Inca, leader of the Inca resistance. He held off the Spanish conquistadors until he was able to escape to the jungle, where he ruled the remaining Incas until he was betrayed and killed.

From where we stood on the terraces we could see the storehouses on the mountainside facing us, where the Incas kept food cool and stored grain. They were the equivalent of our fridges and freezers but it must have been a long hike to get at them, perched high up on the mountain. There was also a face carved out of the rock, supposedly of Wiracocha the sun god. We didn't get to the very top where the houses looked almost as they were when they were occupied. I was beginning to feel dizzy and so we retreated slowly and made our way down to the bus to shut our eyes for ten minutes before everyone joined us. Actually it was impossible to close your eyes. There was too much of interest going on outside. I couldn't take my eyes off the small groups chatting, selling things and generally wandering around in their colourful clothing. On the way back we drove off the road to take photos of snow-capped mountains beyond the rolling fields as the sun slowly sank behind us. At dinner in the hotel we sat at long tables, but again I could not manage to eat anything. Apologising over my untouched soup I crawled upstairs to bed waking every few hours with a raging thirst and headache and sipping bottled water.

In the morning, I awoke feeling fine. Breakfast was lovely, fresh ripe mangoes and croissants with some kind of red berry jam that really tasted wonderful. There was cooked food as well for those who wanted it and tea with long life milk. We had the morning to ourselves and went off to explore Cuzco. First we discovered an internet centre in the corner of a small pharmacy and collected emails. We bought aspirin for one sol (5 sols = £1) from an assistant who spoke good English and was pleasant and helpful. She directed us to the big square in front of the cathedral and immediately child hawkers surrounded us. It was impossible to be cross with them because, although persistent, they were also polite. One lad took us towards the market and chatted as we went. He could speak French he said, and managed one sentence before changing back to his much better English. He knew all about UK football teams and used any knowledge about Britain to keep our attention. He insisted his name was Kevin Keegan until at last he admitted he was really called Diametric. He told us we would not like the market we had asked to see; it was not the tourist market so we decided not to go there because we were short of time. However we had enjoyed talking to him so much that I bought four of his battered postcards.

Outside the cathedral it began to rain heavily and we sheltered on a covered terrace and had our shoes cleaned by a small boy who must have been about eight. He was thin and looked hungry but was warmly dressed. His friend wanted to clean them as well but we had run out of sols. I talked to a young rambler carrying a huge backpack, sheltering like us from the rain with his friends. He was an engineer from Santiago in Chile and was backpacking around Peru. I tried to ask him about altitude sickness but I'm not sure he understood. He seemed in good health, despite the load on his back. I wished, not for the first time, that we could at least speak as much Spanish as we could French. There was a quiet shop just off the square where they sold the usual woollen gear and souvenirs and we bought a rucksack made of the same brightly woven wool material used for clothing. We also bought two soft alpaca scarves for ourselves and wore them for the afternoon tour.

Sacsayhuaman, pronounced 'sexy woman' was a fortress on an immense scale where the Inca King could speak to the thousands of people who came to hear him. It has a double wall in a zigzag shape and Juan Carlos demonstrated how the king's voice could easily be heard anywhere in the huge arena without any amplification. Some of the group stood on one side while the rest of us waited in a corner of the wall. Even though he didn't shout, it was possible to hear his voice from the other side. It seemed to come out of the walls. The Pope also used Sacsayhuaman when he visited Cuzco, but he did not stand on the Inca's throne from where it is said parading troops were reviewed. From here we drove higher with a magnificent view over Cuzco until we came to Tambo Machay, the sacred bathing place for Inca rulers and royal women. Once again eager faces begging us to buy besieged us.

That evening we ate in a restaurant in the main square of Cusco and were entertained with folkloric music. The night's group were very versatile, playing all kinds of pipes and stringed instruments and also conch shells that made a sad mournful sound. Four dancers performed in front of them. At the end of the meal, disappointingly European, I looked out through the upstairs balcony window on to the glittering panorama below. The cathedral and other buildings were illuminated and crowds of people were just walking around enjoying the scene.

Two fires were burning on the steps of the cathedral and when I asked the guide he thought at first it was probably some local folk dancing. Later, when he looked more carefully he realised it was a wedding party. A fire engine blocked the road and firemen in their red uniforms lined the steps while in the middle stood a bride all in white and her new fireman partner. The ceremony was taking place on the steps of the cathedral. The coach driver drove slowly around the square so that we could get a better look. As the rest of the traffic was dawdling along doing the same thing with horns hooting madly we had plenty of time. I would really like to have walked back to the hotel but we were tired and had to get up for an early start the next day. The children were still outside the hotel reminding us to buy. I wished they were safely tucked up at home and wondered if they all had somewhere to sleep.

Next day was the one we had all been waiting for. After an alarm call at 4.15am we had a quick breakfast of fruit and a croissant and scrambled on to the coach. The train left Cuzco at 6am and already as we turned into the station yard, hundreds of Peruvians were busy outside setting up their market stalls. Some must have slept on the pavements all night. The train was smarter than I had expected. Apparently it is a first class train and there are others, second, third and fourth. This one had four or five carriages I think, though we were rushed aboard so quickly that I didn't really have time to look. There were windows in the roof as well as the sides, which meant that as we went into the mountains we had views of their snow-capped tops as we gradually travelled alongside the river in a deep gorge. We left Cuzco and first went forwards then backwards, zigzagging our way up the steep hillside and onto a large plain. On the small farms we could see people already working in the fields, using picks and spades or ploughing with hand ploughs drawn by one ox. Some farms were small but one place near the line had a good herd of cattle penned in, perhaps for milking. On the riverbank I saw a family milking their goats. We passed small villages with ducks and chickens wandering along the narrow gauge railway track, and houses whose doors opened right on to it. Everyone waved and smiled as we passed. Machu Picchu is at a lower altitude than Cusco but it seemed difficult to believe this when we went into the mountains. Juan Carlos pointed out the remains of an Inca settlement on the hillside. The Incas may have used the river to gain access to it because the mountains behind looked completely inaccessible. As we ate a second breakfast on the train he told us the story of Pachacutec, the Inca king responsible for the construction of Machu Picchu in the 15th century. He was a warlike king who, having secured victory over local tribes, looked for a place to build a refuge for himself and other Inca royalty and his elite troops. The fortress he built is surrounded by steep cliffs and secluded from sight by thick jungle. There is only one entry point so it was easy to defend. It was also a place of great spiritual significance to the Inca royalty, a privileged spot to view the heavens and the movements of sun and stars, which were the deities of the Incas. Also nearby, was a quarry supplying white granite of high quality for building so it had everything. Machu Picchu was occupied for three hundred years and then mysteriously abandoned, though no one really seems to know why.

The journey took three and a half hours but the spectacular scenery easily absorbed the time. The stops in between were full of little surprises too. In one halt, not a village at all, a woman came out carrying a huge bunch of lilies, their pure whiteness enhanced against her dark skin. No one wanted to buy the flowers and carry them all day but we gave her some money just to take her photograph with them.

When the train reached its final stop, weary-looking backpackers were waiting on the small platform to go back to Cuzco. We walked down a narrow alley and crossed a bridge over the raging torrent we had been following for miles. On each side of the path rows of tin roofed shacks piled higgledy-piggledy down the hillside with mud roads in between. We hurried past stalls full of more jumpers and hats not wanting to lose sight of Juan Carlos striding ahead of us. There were buses waiting to take us up to the Inca settlement.

Despite the crowds of tourists milling around the smart modern restaurant at the top, it's possible to lose the noise and bustle as you set off on foot along the terraced path. There is a spiritual quality to these ruins that have stood firmly through many earthquakes and were completely covered in jungle greenery when Hiram Bingham, an American anthropologist, found them in 1912. Machu Picchu means 'ancient peak', and indeed the mountain under which the city shelters does look as if it has been there since the beginning of time. Sensitively restored in places just enough to retain the paths and stone staircases, it is easy to recognise buildings. The Temple of the Sun and the storehouses for grain that were grown on the terraces are still there. Water still runs along the stone channels supplying groups of dwellings and irrigating the crops. The gardens used for fruit and flowers are all wild now but still beautiful.

Finally sated with information and needing a break, the Doc and I slipped away for a wander on our own. We climbed the terraces to the remains of a watchtower. Below us the river sparkled in the sun and three llamas grazed on a narrow ledge. Our only other companion, a Japanese woman, sat on the very edge of the mountainside, her camera pressed to her face. Not so far above us fluffy clouds sailed across mountain peaks in a deep blue sky. Squinting slightly to blur one's vision it was possible to peer down and imagine the Machu Picchu of long ago: strong sturdy buildings, the lower ones for farmers and teachers, surrounded by terraces and aqueducts, and the most important religious areas containing the Sacred Plaza and the temples at the crest of the hill overlooking the valley, thousands of feet below. With my squinty eyes the tourists below me could be Inca people going about their business and us, the Doc and me and the Japanese woman, the soldiers on guard above. Regretfully I abandoned my dreaming, and we descended a long stone staircase and joined the others at the entrance.

On the return journey the train steward and the hostess entertained us. First the steward was a clown with a white mask, dancing up and down the aisle and telling jokes. This was followed by a fashion display when both he and the hostess proudly displayed some of the Alpaca woollens we had seen for sale. We thought of telling Virgin and other train companies about this good idea and chuckled to think of their response.

The Seaman's Pocket Book

While writing this, my last story, I asked the Doc to look back and review his shipboard experiences. He had found a book someone gave him for a joke when he first joined the company and it's all about the art of seamanship, and the management and maintenance of ships. Although very old and really meant for sailing ships, it was useful for learning the correct names and terms used on board, though fortunately he never needed to sling his hammock or coil a rope.

Officers and crew were always ready to help and *The Daily Times*, the ship's own newspaper, also gave us both useful snippets of information as well as a programme of daily events. It explained wind speeds as measured on the Beaufort scale and nautical knots about which he was often asked. A knot is a unit of speed measuring one nautical mile per hour. In the days when sailors didn't have modern aids, they threw a weighted log fixed to a rope over the stern. The weight made the log stay upright and sailors believed it stayed in the same place where it had been thrown in. By measuring the length of the rope they found how far the ship had travelled and calculated its speed. They recorded the information in a book predictably named, the log-book. I found all this nautical knowledge very difficult to understand and was better at anticipating and solving minor practical problems.

Once, having been hastily summoned to join the ship at short notice, we set off for Dover without the 'whites' (that's the uniform for cruises in sunny climes). Being certain we would need them we hunted all over Dover for mens' white trousers and white shoes, not easy to find in November. A gentlemens' outfitters finally searched their previous summer's stock and came up with cricket trousers but we couldn't find shoes and had to borrow some from one of the ship's officers.

The first thing the Doc has to do when we go on board is to report to the nurse in charge who is usually waiting for us so that she can get ashore herself for an hour or so before the ship sails. Then there's a meeting with the Safety Officer to collect instructions and if you are new to the ship, a written test of fifty questions on safety. Meanwhile, I'm in our cabin reminding myself of our lifeboat numbers and my muster station. Though we share a cabin, our lives will be necessarily separate for most of the time on board. The Doc starts the day in the Officers' Mess with cereal and orange juice while my breakfasts vary according to the time I get up and where we are in the world. If we are in port, the early morning is a good time for the Doc to meet the port agents who play a vital role in getting patients seen or admitted to hospital as soon as the ship is cleared by port authorities. They will also collect medicines and, importantly for me, know the best places to go for a meal or a drink if we are able to go ashore.

Crew drills depend on the zeal of the First Officer and the Safety Officer but they take place regularly throughout the cruise. They always involve the medical team. The six selected crew-members are trained for emergencies by the nurses and join the Doc at the drills.

Two carry the stretcher, and the four others carry oxygen, defibrillator, suction pump and emergency bag.

The Doc reminded me about a funny incident involving a Staff Captain who had volunteered to be a casualty for the crew drill. He nearly came to grief when it became apparent that he was too large to be lifted through the escape hatch with the tackle and hoist supplied. A series of pushes and pulls had to be applied instead and a very red-faced medical team faced the post drill briefing while the First Officer tried to keep a straight face.

Another drill caused great hilarity because a casualty could not be found anywhere on board. After searching the entire ship several times, it was discovered that signals from another ship in dock on the same radio wave frequency had confused the instructions. The second casualty was, in fact, on board the other cruise ship. This time the medical team could not be blamed.

Morning and evening clinics can be demanding or sometimes quiet and rather boring with little to do except catch up on notes and reading. Some passengers come on board with chronic illnesses and vast quantities of medication. Sometimes they forget their pills and have to be given the nearest equivalent until we reach the next port. Perhaps the most unusual patients are those like the man who came on board with his jaw wired together who had to live on fluids, and a child on permanent oxygen whose father carried it around for him all the time.

In emergencies the choices are limited. The Doc can consider asking the Captain to return to port, divert to another, request a helicopter evacuation, or he can sit tight and wait and see how the situation develops. One day when we had just left port in Bridgetown Barbados, the

Doc went to clinic and I went below to iron my posh frocks. I returned to the cabin half an hour later to find to my astonishment that we were just leaving Bridgetown again. The first patient in the clinic had been a passenger with suspected appendicitis and the ship had returned to port so that he could be taken to hospital.

Infectious diseases are a big problem on board ships and in all areas where there are large numbers of people in a small space. If they become ill on board, passengers are asked to stay in their cabins to try to limit the spread of infection. This suggestion is never very popular, especially as it includes the partner who is not ill. At meal times, a waiter stands at the entrance of every dining room, waiting to spray passengers' hands with antiseptic lotion. Handrails, door handles and banisters are disinfected several times a day, and if there is any illness on board ship, buffet meals have to be served by staff and passengers are not allowed to help themselves. Although rules like this seem very severe, they do seem to be effective.

The evening before we reach a port the Doc is reminded to sign a Maritime Declaration of Health for the Port Authorities, stating that the ship is free of pest, cholera, yellow fever, small pox, typhus, or recurrent fever. Looking over his shoulder at the form one evening, I noticed that it asked if we had any rodents on board. "Have we got rats on board?" I asked a passing waiter. "Yes madam," he replied, smiling. "They were on the menu tonight."

I haven't ever seen any on board ship but I once saw large rats on a quay, scurrying into the late night shadows in a country whose name I've forgotten.

Occasionally passengers use the medical centre as a refuge. One man, who found he was sharing a cabin with an alcoholic stranger who was keeping him awake, decided to sleep on the settee in the waiting room. He crept in late at night in his pyjamas with his duvet and pillow and slept soundly until early morning. Fortunately the situation ended happily when another cabin became available for the rest of his cruise.

The Doc also likes taking care of the crew. They have to have a medical certificate to be allowed not to work, but seldom fake illness because it leaves more work for others. If necessary he can refer them for treatment ashore and it's good to meet them on a later cruise and find everything back to normal. Routine hygiene inspections, throat and hand checks and spot checks on cabins are regular occurrences but he is not usually involved in these.

Two or three staff often share cabins with communal showers and have their meals cooked by their own chef. It's interesting to talk to them about their lives and homes. Many are married with children far away being cared for by grandparents or other relatives. Their spouses are sometimes working on board too but may be on other ships. I found it difficult to imagine living like this and perhaps only meeting my husband once or twice a year! Sometimes we were invited to a crew party below deck and stayed for a short while enjoying the banter until the music got too loud and drove us 'upstairs' again.

Near the end of every cruise, an evening is assigned for crew members to entertain the passengers with a crew show. Hours of rehearsal below deck culminate in a riot of colourful costumes and songs and dances, many from their native countries. I can never watch this show without a lump in my throat as the crew throw their hearts into the final songs in their own language. After this there's a gala buffet when the chefs have a chance to show the extent of their culinary and decorative skills. It's a good opportunity to take photos of the tables groaning with creative food displays and even if I can't eat very much I take home pictures to show friends and make their mouths water.

Not so popular is the regular ritual of 'Officers Dancing'. On one formal evening each cruise the ship's officers assemble in the Lido lounge until summoned to the dance floor by the Captain. The orchestra strikes up and they wait to be invited to dance by lady passengers. Well, actually it is more like a scrum as zealous ladies try to be the first to grab the Captain. Once, deciding that some strategy was needed, the Doc made a prior arrangement with a friend who had come with us on the cruise. As the band began playing and in order to secure him quickly, she shot past the captain and grabbed the Doc first, not done in the best of social circles. Fortunately, this Captain had a sense of humour even when being asked yet again, "Who's steering the ship?" by his dancing partners.

A cruise ship is really a world in miniature with a team of people looking after the needs of more people who have paid to be transported to other parts of the world while being fed and entertained. The crew like to have a bit of fun too and someone once sent a document round by email that made us smile. It was called 'The Real World' and I picked out favourite parts of it to keep:

"In the real world you can come and go, to and fro from your house at any time without the need to sign in or sign out at the front door. It's also possible to walk from your front door to the road or pavement without having to be ferried there in a small boat.

"In the real world you don't have to be back at home one hour before your house starts moving.

"In the real world you don't have to reassure visitors to your house that it's not about to sink simply because it may be a little windy outside.

"In the real world you have the choice of whether or not you want a bed fitted with a ladder.

"In the real world some people work for five days and then have two days off. They start at 9am and finish at 5pm. They do not go to work one morning and return home four or six months later!"

Our cruises don't last that long, of course, but after signing his last report and saying goodbye to everyone, the Doc carries our cases down the gangway and I follow, already hoping there will be another one soon and that he will need me, his social secretary, to go with him.

Acknowledgements

Thank you to all the people who have helped and encouraged me while writing this book.

Special thanks go to Michael Rhodes who read and corrected many initial mistakes and kept prompting me to keep writing when I got discouraged.

I'm grateful to my niece, Chloe, who spared the time to edit the first draft when she was busy studying and working herself, and to Tony McCrum and Sam Jordison who gave me good advice.

Thank you to my sister Christine, who suggested I write the tales in the first place and also my sons Richard, Chris and Steve and all my family and friends. Extra special thanks go to my husband, Selwyn, who made it all possible.

Having travelled on four of their cruise ships, I will always be grateful to Fred Olsen Cruise Lines for the opportunity of seeing so many wonderful and very different parts of the world and for their permission for the use of photographs and the services of Rachel Jackson, their publicity officer. I would also like to thank all the officers and crew who went out of their way to make me welcome on board and gave us help and advice, especially the Nurses.

Finally, to Troubador Publishing for helping me in all the details concerned with putting the book together.